Low-Fat Love

SOCIAL FICTIONS SERIES
Volume 1

Series Editor
Patricia Leavy
Stonehill College

The Social Fictions series emerges out of the arts-based research movement. The series includes full-length fiction books that are informed by social research but written in a literary/artistic form (novels, plays, and short story collections). Believing there is much to learn through fiction, the series only includes works written entirely in the literary medium adapted. Each book includes an academic introduction that explains the research and teaching that informs the book as well as how the book can be used in college courses. The books are underscored with social science or other scholarly perspectives and intended to be relevant to the lives of college students—to tap into important issues in the unique ways that artistic or literary forms can.

Please email queries to pleavy7@aol.com

International Editorial Advisory Board

Low-Fat Love

Patricia Leavy
Stonehill College, USA

SENSE PUBLISHERS
ROTTERDAM/BOSTON/TAIPEI

A C.I.P. record for this book is available from the Library of Congress.

ISBN: 978-94-6091-646-5 (paperback)
ISBN: 978-94-6091-647-2 (hardback)
ISBN: 978-94-6091-648-9 (e-book)

Published by: Sense Publishers,
P.O. Box 21858,
3001 AW Rotterdam,
The Netherlands
www.sensepublishers.com

Printed on acid-free paper

DEDICATION

For Mark Robins, with love

TABLE OF CONTENTS

Acknowledgments ix

Preface xi

Part One
Chapter 1 3
Chapter 2 21
Chapter 3 29
Chapter 4 39
Chapter 5 55

Part Two
Chapter 6 79
Chapter 7 91
Chapter 8 95
Chapter 9 99
Chapter 10 105
Chapter 11 109
Chapter 12 127
Chapter 13 137

Part Three
Chapter 14 145
Chapter 15 149
Chapter 16 153
Chapter 17 169
Chapter 18 183

About the Author 189

ACKNOWLEDGMENTS

First and foremost, thank you to my publisher, Peter de Liefde, for your willingness to innovate. I am grateful to you and the entire team at Sense Publishers, particularly Bernice Kelly for your production assistance. Likewise, thank you to Mitch Allen and Lori Handelman for your wisdom and encouragement. I extend a heartfelt note of gratitude to my colleagues and the administration at Stonehill College for all the support as I continue to carve my professional identity. Carolyn Ellis and Art Bochner: I was lucky to take a workshop with you at the beginning of this writing journey—thank you for teaching me the importance of vulnerability. Thank you to the editorial advisory board members of the *Social Fictions* series for your ingenuity, generosity and support. Tori Amos, thank you for being my musical muse: for this book I walked through the fire and "made my own *Pretty Hate Machine*." I extend my deepest gratitude to the many women who have shared their stories with me over the years. These pages are also peopled with the ghosts of relationships past, and I am thankful to all those who haunt the pages. I have learned from each of you. I am also grateful to my close female friends whose humor and wisdom make their way onto these pages— you know who you are. As always, thank you to my parents for your love and friendship. A special hug to my mother: thank you for encouraging me to write and for wanting this book to happen for so many years. Thank you also to the best in-laws one could hope for, Carolyn and Charles Robins. Mostly importantly, thank you to my great loves, Madeline and Mark: your love is the real-deal, full fat, and allows me to live a big life! Mark, this is for you.

PREFACE

Low-Fat Love unfolds over three seasons as Prilly Greene and Janice Goldwyn, adversarial editors at a New York press, experience personal change relating to the men (and absence of women) in their lives. Ultimately, each woman is pushed to confront her own image of herself, exploring her insecurities, the stagnation in her life, her attraction to men who withhold their support and her reasons for having settled for low-fat love.

Prilly lives in between who she is and who she longs to be. Prilly falls for Pete Rice, an unemployed, ever-sexy and curiously charming aspiring graphic novelist. Prilly thinks she is finally experiencing the big life she always sought but feared was beyond her grasp because she was "in the middle" (not beautiful or ugly, not greatly talented or totally hopeless—someone who could work for it). Pete's unconventional, free-spirited views on relationships unsettle Prilly, ultimately causing her to unravel over the course of their on-again-off-again love affair. Meanwhile, Janice, a workaholic, feminist in-name-only editor, overburdens Prilly, her underling, with busywork and undercuts Prilly's professional identity. Janice's regimented life is set on a new course when her alcoholic father becomes injured in a car accident and she is forced to face her own demons.

Along with Prilly and Janice, a cast of characters' stories are interwoven throughout and eventually connected in the third and final section of the book. The offbeat characters include: Melville Wicket, Pete's awkward friend who lives one beat outside of the moment; Jacob, Melville's younger, pothead brother; Kyle Goldwyn, Janice's 17 year old son who appears ordinary in every way but is actually quite extraordinary; and Tash, Kyle's wild-child, flighty sexpot cousin who attends NYU and ends up dating Jacob. In the end, momentum builds as the characters struggle to escape the consequences of their decisions. Unexpected events cause changes in the characters that appear minor—but that carry significant implications for their futures.

Low-Fat Love is underscored with a commentary about female identity-building and self-acceptance and how, too often, women become trapped in limited visions of themselves. Women's media is used as a signpost throughout the book in order to make visible the context in which women come to think of themselves as well as the men and women in their lives. In this respect *Low-Fat Love* offers a critical commentary about popular culture and the social construction of femininity. Ultimately, the book explores women's identity struggles in relation to the men in their lives and how women often develop myopic images of themselves as a part of "face-saving" strategies employed to cover up shame and a learned devaluation of self. *Low-Fat Love* suggests women seek new ways to see that are not dependent on male approval so that they will value themselves and reject degrading relationships. Moreover, as the main characters in the book learn, the most toxic relationship a woman may participate in is often with herself. So, too, the men in *Low-Fat Love* learn that one must find one's voice or suffer the consequences.

Low-Fat Love is grounded in a decade of research and teaching about gender, relationships and popular culture, which informs the pop-feminist undertone of the book. Over the past decade, I have conducted numerous interviews with young women about their relationships, body image, sexual and gender identities. Additionally, I have taught many college courses on the sociology of gender, critical approaches to popular culture and human sexuality and intimacy. These courses have sparked wonderful discussions with my students about identity. All of these experiences and conversations informed the writing of this book. Moreover, my own personal experiences, although fictionalized, are interwoven into the words that follow (a practice qualitative researchers refer to as autoethnography). In these ways, *Low-Fat Love* emerges out of the arts-based research movement in the qualitative research community and seeks to fictionalize and chronicle the experiences of countless interviewees, students and friends, as well as my own experiences. In this respect, the book represents an a/r/tographical rendering—a work in which I have merged my artist-researcher-teacher identities. As a novel, *Low-Fat Love* can be read purely for pleasure or used in a variety of courses in women's/gender studies, sociology, popular culture, media studies, communications, qualitative research and arts-based research. I hope the book resonates with readers and provides a springboard for self-reflection or discussion.

Patricia Leavy

PART ONE

"'Casey bombed into town with her daily organizer.' It's the worst first line I've ever heard! I mean, you're left with this organizer, just sitting there, for no reason. You never mention something so irrelevant right in the beginning. It's awful. Nowadays everyone thinks they can write. There are no real writers anymore," he said, flinging the manuscript on Prilly's desk.

"Just real editors, right Stuart?"

"Ah, you're just soft Prilly. You can't coddle them. There's no point."

With a friendly roll of the eyes she agreed to the inevitable. "I know, I know," she said shaking her head. "I'll tell him we can't go forward with publication."

"Good. We've got to start streamlining our list. Bad writing that sells millions of copies is one thing, but unsuccessful bad writing is an embarrassment. And I don't have to remind you that we can't afford the drain."

Prilly smiled, thinking his remark about unsuccessful bad writing was dead-on. "Got it. I'll take care of it."

Stuart left her small, drab office, inadvertently knocking a teetering stack of mail off the corner of her desk. The piles on her desk taunted her. She desperately desired to have everything organized and in its place, but she just couldn't manage it for more than a couple of days at a time. She had seen an episode of Oprah where an expert said that clutter in one's office or home meant clutter in one's emotional and spiritual life. As she wondered whether that was true, she reread the beginning of the manuscript. Was it really such a bad opening line?

*

That night when Prilly entered her apartment she immediately kicked off her comfort heels and slipped on her at-home uniform: Old Navy black pajama pants and worn out Ugg boots. She poured a glass of Beaujolais and lay on the couch. Remote in hand, she flipped between her usual stations and landed on "Access Hollywood." They were featuring a story about Brad Pitt and Angelina Jolie. She always bought tabloids when they were on the cover. Although she despised the idea that they were mostly adored for their good looks, she too was fascinated. Sometimes she would fantasize about what Angelina's life was like. Of all the celebrities, Angelina seemed to have it all. She was ridiculously gorgeous, the kind of beauty that doesn't seem to go out of style, or to age. She had lived a wild life, and now she had a massive multicultural family (that she probably never had to take care of with all her nannies, assistants and so forth), a fabulous partner who undoubtedly worshipped her, and an amazing career. Somehow she had managed to be both an artist and a commercial success, or at least she could reasonably claim to be both. People admired her. People like Prilly. As Prilly watched the story she felt a familiar storm cloud of envy, longing, and self-loathing.

"Access Hollywood" was just the prelude to whatever "movie of the week" she could find. Tonight she was watching a Lifetime movie about a woman who worked as a newspaper reporter and, while reporting on a local crime, became the next target of a psychopath. As she picked up each forkful of the vegetable stir fry she made during the commercials, she couldn't help but think that in some ways the reporter was lucky. At least her life was exciting.

Prilly lived in between who she was and who she wanted to be. She had moved to Manhattan from Boston in search of a *big life*. She had always felt she was meant to have a *big life*. To date, she had barely had a small life. Although she was an atheist, like many other atheists she blamed God for all her problems (at least when she wasn't blaming her parents). She thought it all came down to looks, to genetics. She was convinced that beautiful people have a much greater shot at a big life. Ugly people have no shot. People somewhere in the middle, which is where she was firmly located, had to work hard for it, but it *was* possible. So ever since Prilly was about seven years old and she figured out that she was regular looking at best, she blamed God and her parents for her lot in life. As a teenager she admired the beautiful, popular girls. To her, they had been graced with the best gift of all, the gift of possibility. When you were beautiful, all you had to do was add on to that to get what you want, to be who you want to be. When you weren't beautiful, you spent your life making up for it, filling in what was lacking. Compensating. At times Prilly even envied the ugly girls. If you were ugly and knew it, there was no hope of a big life and so ultimately that would be very freeing. You could focus on being content with your life as it was. Ugly girls didn't have to waste time or money with makeup, hair care, exercise, beauty treatments and fashion. What was the point? No one fabulous would ever get close enough to reject them, so they must be free from disappointment too, she thought -- at least once they accepted their situation. The ones who had it the worst were those in the middle; the girls who, with enough work could be considered pretty, but never beautiful. Those girls had it the worst because they could taste the big life, they could see it close enough to want it, to reach for it. Prilly was in the middle.

*

Pete Rice had just picked up the latest Neil Gaiman book and planned to spend the next several hours reading it while drinking dark roast coffee. He loved the smell of coffee brewing. It was his favorite smell.

As Pete waited for the coffee to brew, he replayed the scene of Rachel storming out of his apartment the night before. He decided not to call her; he didn't care. He had a theory about women. If they loved you, you could control them. But if they loved you too much, disaster. He had had disasters. (There was Alice who showed up to a party at his friend's house, plastered, shouting that he had an STD. He didn't. Then there was the catalogue model, Georgia, who slashed his vintage T-shirt collection and trashed his apartment. This, of course, brings to mind Sophie, who upon catching him in bed with Georgia, used his dirty clothes to make a bonfire on the fire escape outside of his apartment. Worst of all was Sadie who would stake out his usual haunts—a local teahouse, a sandwich shop, a pub— waiting to see him arm-and-arm with another woman which would cause her to scream publicly as if the world was burning and only she could see it. Interestingly, this would cause the woman currently with Pete, in her guiltiest of thoughts, to want him all the more.)

Pete's days depended primarily on three factors: whether or not he was screwing someone steadily (steadily for him being a long series of intense relationships that lasted about two months each), whether or not he had been out all night (he had a penchant for dance clubs, though at 38 he was nearly two decades older than everyone else there), and whether or not he was working (although he resisted any kind of long-term commitment or "career" that would interfere with his art, he did take very occasional part-time jobs ranging from telemarketing to working in a one-hour photo shop, which also never lasted for more than two months). He also vacillated between feeling invincible (he had an "unknown genius" complex, one that was imprinted with the arrogance of a guy who was better looking than behaved) and feeling utterly depressed. That day Pete had expected to be alone.

His studio apartment consisted of one small room that served as his bedroom and workspace, a kitchenette with a cut-out wall that looked into the bedroom, and a small hallway that led to the bathroom and front door. The main room had two large windows, one of which led out to a small fire escape that he used as a teeny tiny porch. Sometimes he grew pot out there, but it was usually stolen by his neighbors.

He used an old queen size mattress and box spring, but no bed frame, so his bed was low down on the floor. Gaiman book in hand, he propped up two pillows against the white stucco wall and sat down wearing his black and white checkered boxers and an old David Bowie T-shirt. He placed his oversized "I Love NY" mug on the cinderblock to the right of his bed, and opened the book. He always read the dedication first. He felt you could learn everything about the soul of an author by reading the dedication page and, thus, the soul of the book. Books without dedications always disappointed him. Just as he flipped to the first page there was a knock on his front door.

He walked to the door and shouted, "Who is it?"

"Melville."

Pete opened the door. Neither said a word, and Pete just walked back down his narrow hallway to his bedroom while pulling at a wedgie. Melville locked the door and followed. Pete plopped down on his mattress and picked up his coffee. Melville pulled out the rolling computer chair tucked under the desk opposite the bed. He turned it to face Pete and sat down. Then he stood up and took off his jacket and sat down again, placing the orange garment across his lap.

"So what's up?"

"Oh, nothing, I was downtown visiting my cousin so I thought I'd stop in. I thought maybe we could get some coffee or something. What are you doing?"

"Nothing. I got the new Gaiman book and I was just going to start it."

"I could have gotten you a deal on that. I hope you didn't pay full price, not for the hardcover. I know a store where you can get hard covers half off, even new ones. If you get 'em used you can get them for a few bucks. Hard covers are a rip off anyway."

As Melville was talking, slowly as ever, Pete wished that he would shut up. He was the cheapest person he had ever met. He had holes in his sweaters and had sported the same worn out ugly orange windbreaker for the whole time Pete had known him— more than a decade. Pete hated going out to eat with him because Melville would refuse to tip appropriately. He would leave spare change, usually about a 4% tip at the most. Pete was cheap too, but only privately. In public he intentionally gave the impression of being generous but in private, he would often screw friends who loaned him money, haggle with the landlord over the rent if there was any minor repair needed in the apartment (real or imagined), and while he always had money for expensive restaurants, liquor, books, art supplies and all things entertainment, he never seemed to have money for anything else. For example, he had no health, dental or life insurance. Nor did he have any property (beyond the books and odds and ends in his tiny rented apartment). He routinely bought an overpriced cappuccino from the café down the street, only to drink a sip and then put it to the side where he would forget about it, but he couldn't manage to pay his utilities on time and consistently ended up paying late fees and even reinstallation charges. As the flaws in others are always much more apparent than those in ourselves, Pete was oblivious. He wished that Melville wasn't so cheap or at least that he'd have the sense to shut up about it. The truth was, he was embarrassed to be friends with Melville. Pete prided himself on chasing the muse, being in tune with the zeitgeist, and living in the moment. To Pete, Melville was the embodiment of all that he disdained. Pete decided that Melville lived one beat outside the moment. That was why he was so slow relaying the simplest of information and why, at the age of 36, Pete suspected he may still be a virgin. Yet despite his harsh evaluation of Melville, he remained the only reliable presence in Pete's life.

Totally ignoring Melville's inane hardcover commentary, Pete shot back with, "Yeah, ok, let's go grab a bite. I need to shower. You can make yourself some coffee if you want. I'm out of filters but there's paper toweling there. Flip through that book, or look in that folder over there," he said, pointing to a pile of papers on the desk behind Melville. "I've expanded the carnival part of the story and I'd like to know what you think. No one's read it yet. You're in for a treat."

"I'll be out in a jiff," Pete hollered as he walked into the bathroom, coffee mug in hand.

Forty-five minutes later they were sitting down in a diner three blocks away. Pete was an inconsistent regular. He would go through spurts of eating there nearly every day, sometimes more than once a day, and other times he wouldn't go for months at a time. Just as any given waitress was getting to know him, he'd take a hiatus and she'd forget him by the time he returned. When the waitress came to take their order, Pete couldn't help but notice how unusual looking she was. He had a knack for noticing atypical faces, and this face intrigued him. It was fairly old but probably appeared older than its biological age. It had very long features and a strong nose. After further examination he determined that the nose was in fact so ugly that he actually found it quite wonderful. He expected an interesting accent to match the face, but when she said, "What'll it be?" it was with the same New York accent he had come to tire of in the last five of the fifteen years he had been in the States.

"I'll have two eggs over easy with wheat toast. I'd like marmalade on the side, not jam. And coffee, with cream."

"And you?" she asked looking at Melville who was still staring directly into the oversized plastic laminated menu.

"Um, what does the special egg sandwich come with?"

"Homefries."

"Does it come with a drink?"

"No, just homefries."

"Um, ok, I'll have that."

"Something to drink?"

"Just water."

Pete, growing tired of these uncomfortable exchanges, had occupied himself by doodling in the small notepad he always carried with him. By the time Melville looked up from his menu, Pete was in another world.

"So I read the new pages."

"Yeah, and?" Pete asked both eager to hear the response and annoyed that he had to coax it out of him.

"They're good but you're missing some commas in a couple of places. I can show you where." (Melville had been an English major in college, until he dropped out sophomore year.)

"Commas? Fucking commas? This is your insight? I don't give a fuck about commas! I hate fucking commas. Do you have anything useful to contribute or are you just taking up space?"

Although hurt by Pete's patronizing rant, Melville ignored it as he was accustomed to doing. Wanting to show Pete he had more to offer, that he wasn't just "taking up space," he quickly retorted, "Well I don't get where you are going with the main character. The writing is good but there's nowhere to take it."

"Ha! You should stick to commas," Pete said through hearty laughter.

Melville shrugged, looking down. Although Pete had never noticed, Melville never looked him in the eyes. Never. He normally looked down and sometimes to the side.

"You'll get it when it's all there. That's your problem, you need it all spelled out. Can't feeeeel where it's headin'. But don't worry, it'll all be there and you'll get it."

With that the waitress brought breakfast. Melville ate swiftly, looking down at his food the entire time. Pete spent a few minutes dunking the corner of his toast into his egg yolks before eating.

At the end of the meal there was some typical squabbling about the bill. Melville left his usual 4% tip. Anyone else would have just thrown some extra money down but Pete, being secretly cheap himself, guilted Melville into putting down a couple of dollars. Pete either didn't realize or care that when Melville gave in it was just to get Pete to shut up. He couldn't stand the sound of his voice. Although Melville envied him, particularly with women, he also found Pete laborious. Walking out, Pete noticed a flyer in the entrance of the diner. It announced a book reading by Jeanette Winterson that Saturday afternoon at a local book store. He ripped down the flyer and said, "We should go to this. It would be good for you to hear a real writer. No one uses metaphor quite like Winterson. She's good."

Not acknowledging the condemnation, Melville simply replied, "Yeah, ok."

*

On the train Melville Wicket sat still and silent. Only weeks before he had moved into his younger brother Jacob's apartment in Brooklyn, which he shared with a manic depressive named Jeremy.

Melville was a telemarketer for a medical insurance company. He only worked 28 hours a week so his employer could get away without paying him benefits, like medical insurance. With hardly enough income to live, Melville had been staying in a small basement room in a rooming house for the past three years. He paid month-to-month. Some residents had week-to-week deals. The room was half above ground and half below. There were two small rectangular windows high on the right wall, nearly touching the ceiling, with rusty iron bars. Underneath there was a small refrigerator, the kind you would expect to find in a college dorm room, a microwave, and an electric Crock-Pot that violated building codes. Across from the windows there was a twin size bed with old off white sheets, one flattened pillow, and a worn out queen sized down comforter with a few holes. Sometimes when Melville woke up in the morning, there would be feathers in his hair. In his mind he called them chicken feathers. To the left of the bed was a small unfinished wood desk and brown leather chair. On the desk, a stack of library books, a few pieces of old mail, notebooks and pens, an old word processor from 1995, and a small alarm clock with a CD player. On the floor beneath, stacks of CDs. To the right, a tall halogen lamp. There was a shared bathroom in the hallway. Melville was allotted one shelf in the medicine cabinet for his personal items, which he used, although he didn't feel good about it.

Melville would have stayed there forever, but he was asked to leave at the end of the previous month. One of the female residents complained to the Super that Melville had been peeping on her while she was in the bathroom. She claimed that she saw him through the slit of the barely-opened door, a door she claimed to have closed, that he must have pushed ever so slightly open. Two years earlier another woman had made a similar complaint. Melville had denied it, in his usual quiet manner. The Super took pity on him and let him stay, but now with a second complaint, he was out. When he told Pete what happened Pete said, "Spying, you were spying on the girls? Ha!" Melville insisted he hadn't done it, and Pete rolled his eyes but didn't say anything else. He always assumed that Melville was guilty but not because he was a pervert, just because he was shy, and awkward, and terribly lonely.

Jacob hadn't wanted Melville to move in with him, but what could he do, the guy was basically homeless, and he *was* his brother. Besides, he could get money for rent and utilities, leaving more money for pot and the occasional celebratory mushroom. Jacob was 24 and worked in what he called a "vintage music store" in the Village, near Washington Square Park. It was a store that sold rare vinyl and also used CDs, dealing largely in trade. Melville wondered how in the age of Ebay and Itunes a store like that could stay in business. When he once asked Jacob about it, Jacob told him to "shut the fuck up." Melville never mentioned it again. Melville didn't know what Jeremy did for a living. Most days he would be in his room all day, sleeping, Melville assumed. But every Tuesday he was up and out of the house by 8:00 am and didn't return until after 6:00 pm. Melville didn't ask questions.

After spending the morning with Pete, Melville returned to his apartment at 3:00 pm. He went straight into his small bedroom. In actuality it was a two bedroom apartment, with a small living room and kitchenette combo room, and one tiny bathroom with a stall shower. The apartment also had a very small sunroom that Jacob turned into a makeshift bedroom for his brother. With no room for a bed, Melville slept on a small couch. The room was very drafty, and Melville was worried about winter. He thought about it all the time. On that day, as most, he entered his room, took off his sneakers, and put on a Puccini CD. He lay on his couch with his jacket still on, listening.

*

Prilly's search for a big life hadn't amounted to much. She was in her office from 8:00 am until 6:30 pm every weekday. By the time she got back to her apartment, it was time for "Access Hollywood" and a healthy dinner, followed by a bad junk food binge with a side of guilt and a movie about women who steal other women's babies or who murder their young repairmen lovers. Although she had been in New York for several years, she hadn't managed to make more than a couple of friends. And she didn't really like them. Much like the fat girl in high school whom she befriended, this, for now, was the best she could do. The single women at work routinely went to local bars together, and, although they always invited her, she never once went. She didn't feel comfortable and thought it would be awful.

After a while she also noticed that they didn't so much invite her, but rather state, "We're heading to Maxwells." She assumed she was welcome to join them; else why would they bother to announce where they were going. But she wasn't sure.

She did take one stab at Internet dating. The Internet appealed to her for two main reasons. First, no one had to know about it. So if it didn't work out she wouldn't have to explain it to anyone. Second, she could screen the men on the basis of income, education, looks and interests. She wanted a man who earned more money than she did, not because she had any intention of becoming dependent on a man, but because it would be hard to have a big life in Manhattan without more money, and a lot of it. She also really wanted to get out of her mounting credit card debt which weighed on her, particularly on the nights she drank a lot. She hoped to meet someone interested in the arts, who could take her to the best shows. Although she wanted to be with a good looking man, which she felt made a so-so looking woman seem much more attractive, she didn't want to be with a man that was too good looking. Men like that always eventually left average women. It was hard to fool them into thinking you were prettier than you actually were. If she managed to get a decent man and turn it into a steady thing, she didn't want to have to do it all over again someday. She also feared being a part of a couple that made other women look and wonder: "What is he doing with her?" The Internet dating ended up costing her $199.00, a weekend's worth of screening time, one terrible evening, and an untold sum of shame. She had made a date with Henry. He seemed promising. He was an accountant who owned his own apartment and claimed to see every foreign film that came out. They were to meet at a Spanish tapas restaurant a few blocks from where she worked for a drink and quick bite. She thought about the date incessantly for five days. She got a manicure, bikini wax and bought two new outfits (neither of which she wore; she decided one was weird and the other looked too "datey"). The night they were supposed to meet she got to the restaurant, stood outside for a minute panicking, walked around the block, and then decided that if he had seen her walk around the block he would already think she was a freak. She went home, drank nearly a bottle of wine, and watched four hours of a nine hour "Murder She Wrote" marathon on the Hallmark channel. Henry sent her an email the next morning asking what had happened and if she was ok. She never responded and took her profile off of Match.com immediately. She felt guilty for months, thinking of Henry often.

Without many friends to go out with, and no real effort at dating, her life had become fairly lonely. She decided to invest energy into her weekend routine. Convinced that if you lead an interesting life you will meet interesting people, Prilly made being interesting her full-time weekend occupation. For her, there was nothing more interesting than the arts. Had she been braver, she might have been some sort of artist, or at least a journalist. She took to surrounding herself with the products of others' bliss. The monotony of the work week was soon juxtaposed to weekends of ballet, theater, concerts, gallery openings, craft markets, spoken word performances, independent films, museums and poetry readings. It was exhausting.

*

"Well I wanted to tell you in person. I know it's difficult but please don't take it personally. We're a mid-sized press and we need to be very careful about what books to publish, particularly for our trade market. Usually we don't even consider unsolicited works."

"But you've sold fifteen thousand copies of my last book. That should count for something. That's why I came to you first. I just don't understand this. Isn't there anything I can do?"

"Yes, I understand how you must feel," Prilly responded in a hushed tone, "but that was an introductory geography textbook, it was an academic printing with a built-in audience we could market too. If you talk with Marcy I'm sure she can explain it to you. The trade market is very different and we publish very few new fiction authors each year. I'm sorry but we can't go with this and I don't want to waste your time. I encourage you to submit it elsewhere."

After a moment of silence in which Prilly could hear her own breath Charles matter-of-factly said, "Well I'm very disappointed. Very disappointed."

With that the large, pear-shaped man got up, outstretched his arm over Prilly's desk for a sweaty handshake, and left.

Prilly felt awful. Normally she would just send rejection emails or letters. She never had to see the person she was rejecting, but because Charles was already published with the house, Stuart had suggested she do it in person next time Charles stopped by to see Marcy, the geography editor.

Just before Prilly could regroup from that experience, Janice popped her head in her door, left ajar by Charles. Just the sight of Janice made Prilly crave Advil.

Janice was a long-time acquisitions editor with the press and Prilly had been her assistant for nine months before being promoted to editor. It was the longest nine months of her life. At first she thought she was incredibly lucky. She was told that there were very few women in publishing who had made it to Janice's level, with her list of accomplishments. After ten years of working in their geography division Janice was given a new list to build, history, a market the press had never ventured into before. With a degree in history Janice had purportedly been thrilled. She had introduced herself to Prilly as a feminist. She boldly said, "Prilly, this is a male dominated industry. It's not easy. But it can be done and we have to support each other." She also prided herself on including women's history and Black history in her line, books she swore other editors would pass by.

Prilly soon found out that feminism was more of a conceptual with Janice. She really enjoyed talking about supporting "women's issues" but she didn't support *actual women*. In fact, over time Prilly learned that Janice was particularly harsh on the women she worked with out of some irrational fear that they would become more successful than her, and what's worse, that they wouldn't have to work as hard to do it. Janice had to work for everything she had, and unlike the "anorexic bitches" she went to college with, she scraped for everything she got, including her education. As a result Janice only liked women beneath her, those that she could easily manipulate and therefore control.

Janice had liked Prilly well enough at first but, when she realized that Prilly wouldn't be content being an assistant forever, she began to grow weary. This weariness led to a quiet resentment. During those days Prilly would often find herself working outrageously long hours that mostly consisted of doing secretarial work for Janice, which was not in Prilly's job description. Assigning these kinds of tasks helped Janice on two levels. First, it made it clear to Prilly and anyone else paying attention that she was in charge, she was Prilly's boss. Second, and even more importantly, it prevented Prilly from doing the kind of work that the publishers would notice, the kind of work that would get Prilly promoted. What Janice failed to recognize was that the publishers had always intended Prilly for an editorial position. They just made her an assistant first so the others wouldn't complain that there was too much rank jumping. When Prilly was promoted she immediately went to Janice, hoping to avoid future unpleasantness, and said, "Thank you so much. Without your mentorship this never would have happened." To this Janice replied in her usual quiet and monotone voice, "Well, actually I did put in a good word for you too. I had to push for this. I had to make this happen. But you deserve it." Prilly thanked her although she knew it wasn't true. In fact she suspected that Janice secretly gave her mediocre performance reviews so that she would remain her assistant indefinitely. Ever since, Janice went out of her way to be nice to Prilly, so much so that it alarmed her. But once in a while, Janice found a way to say something cutting, under the guise of being helpful, like the knock about having to convince the bosses to promote her. It was no wonder that the mere sight of Janice at her door caused a sharp pain in her spine.

"Hi Prilly. What was that about? Charles Pruit looked pretty upset when he left. He used to be one of my authors you know."

Prilly relaxed a bit, hoping Janice was just nosing around for gossip as she was prone to do, and didn't in fact want anything from her beyond chitchat.

"Oh, that's right. He's one of Marcy's now. Same old, same old: he's an academic who thinks he can also be a novelist. I had to tell him that his manuscript isn't for us. He took it pretty hard but... what can you do, you know."

At this Janice shimmied her way into the doorway, allowing her back to gently tap the door closed as if unintentionally. "Oh great," Prilly thought, "There's more."

"Do you want to come in and sit down?" Prilly asked entirely out of obligation.

"Oh sure, just for a minute."

Prilly noticed how Janice always had a way of making things seem like they were someone else's idea, and like *she* was doing *you* a favor.

"Prilly, I wanted to run something by you."

"Sure, what's up?"

"I want to build a list of memoirs, focusing mostly on unknown female authors."

"That sounds great Janice, you should give Stuart a proposal."

"Well I did actually, and that's where you come in. Stuart said that memoirs would fall under your list, that they're sold as trade books and since we don't publish non-fiction trade, they'd have to be a part of our current trade list. He thought it would make sense for someone in your division to partner up with me."

"Hmmm."

"So I suggested that you and I work on it together. We could do it as a book series, instead of a line, at least as a sort of pilot test. If we solicit authors who have already drafted manuscripts we could premier at Trade Launch this Spring. You and I could serve as co-editors-n-chief for the series, with my name listed first. If it does well, we could eventually build a full line. I think this would be an excellent opportunity for you."

"Yeah, I bet you do," Prilly thought to herself. She had learned long ago that Janice only cared about opportunities for herself. Anytime she framed something as an opportunity for someone else, Prilly thought that poor soul should run like the wind. In Prilly's case, there was a part of her that actually liked Janice, despite all the obvious reasons not to. At times Prilly even thought that her fondness for Janice grew in direct proportion to Janice's manipulative behavior. Although she was very different from Janice, deep down she knew that there was a part of them that was the same. A part of each of them that had been shafted and was clawing their way out the best way they knew how; it was just that Janice's claws were sharper. She also wanted to believe in Janice's tale of great feminist heroism in publishing, even though she knew it was a lie. If Janice would just be more forthright, Prilly could even be friends with her. She kept this thought to herself.

"Well it does sound interesting. Why don't you give me your proposal and I'll look over it and we can talk more. I'm really swamped as it is, but I'll definitely look over what you have."

"I'm telling you, this is a great opportunity for you. In fact, Stuart didn't think you were up for it yet but with my convincing, he's willing to give you a shot."

"Well I appreciate that," Prilly said, the way a child thanks their parents when they're given socks for Christmas. "It sounds like a great opportunity but I'd like to look over the specifics and think about it."

Janice couldn't conceal her irritation as she fiddled with her pin-straight light brown hair, but she played along. "Ok, I'll email you the proposal and Stu's notes; we can talk about it early next week."

"Ok, great, thanks Janice."

And with that, Janice left her office, shutting the door behind her. Prilly took four Advil immediately.

*

The weekend couldn't come fast enough for Prilly. She spent Friday night at home with half a bottle of red wine and Chinese takeout. (She always ate right out of the container with the disposable chopsticks. She thought it was more sophisticated even though no one was there to see it, and even though she had no idea how to use chopsticks properly so food invariably dribbled on her couch. This also prevented her from ordering the veggie fried rice she liked, she couldn't possibly eat rice with chopsticks). Saturday she woke up late with a wine-MSG headache and took two Advil.

With no plans until Sunday (when she was meeting an old friend for a several times rescheduled lunch) she sipped her French roast while perusing one of her favorite New York websites, which listed things of interest. Jeanette Winterson was doing a book reading and signing at 4:00 pm. The bookstore was near the shoe repair store where she had left her silver shoes for heel reinforcement. Prilly liked to multitask plus she thought there were sure to be interesting people at the book reading.

"Hang on a minute. Fuck, Melville's banging on the damn door. No, we're going to a book reading. I'm not even dressed so I better get movin. I'll call you later. Hang in there. Bye."

When Pete hung up the phone he stammered down his hallway and opened the door. He turned around and walked back to kitchenette without saying a word. Melville shut the door and followed.

"Christ, I was on the phone. Can't you wait a minute?" Pete asked with a tone that made it clear he was not looking for an answer. "I'm making coffee, do you want some?"

"No thanks," Melville said as he grabbed a comic book off of Pete's desk and sat in the chair, flipping through its pages. Melville didn't care for comic books; he thought they were juvenile and beneath him, but, like so many other thoughts, he kept this to himself.

"I just need to throw my clothes on. I'll bring the coffee to go."

"Ok," Melville said as he started to read a random page in the middle of the comic book.

*

The bookstore was crowded and by the time Pete and Melville got there, fifteen minutes late (though Winterson hadn't begun her reading yet), there weren't any seats left. Melville was secretly annoyed that Pete, per usual, hadn't been ready on time. They stood in the back, leaning against a wall. Pete, burnt out from a sleepless night, sipped his coffee steadily.

When Winterson appeared, everyone stood up and began clapping ferociously. She began by talking about her new work, from which she read several passages. She then took questions from the audience about her first novel *Oranges Are Not the Only Fruit* and fan favorites like *Sexing the Cherry*. Prilly, sitting in the corner of the back row, hadn't read any of Winterson's books; although, she owned several. They were amidst the collection of "important artistic works" she thought everyone should own... and someday even read.

At the end of the question period, there was a book signing. The mob scurried to the front forming a swerving line through the store. Prilly detested standing in lines. Also, she hadn't brought any books with her and wasn't committed to buying the new book. She picked up her unmarked brown paper bag that contained her newly repaired shoes and turned to head out. The bag didn't have a handle and was thus cumbersome. She had to stick it under one of her arms and throw her handbag on her opposite shoulder. She fumbled a bit as she made her way past the rows of arranged chairs towards the door. Melville, still leaning against the wall with Pete, noticed her immediately. She was lovely, he thought. It was his irrepressible staring that made Pete aware of her. As Prilly walked by, Pete said, "You're not getting a book?"

"I'm sorry; did you say something to me?" Prilly asked, catching a glimpse of Pete for the first time. He had striking teal eyes framed with a few soft lines that made her think he had "really lived."

"I just asked if you were getting a book; everyone else seems to be."

"Oh," noticing how sexy his voice was. "The line is too long."

"My friend and I were going to go get a coffee, to talk about the reading. Would you like to join us?"

Stunned by the invitation from a tall, dark-haired man whose name she didn't yet know, Prilly stammered. Pete quickly responded, "It's ok, no worries, but if you're not busy come along."

With that, Pete walked in front of Prilly, opened the door, and let her pass through. He then stepped outside with Melville following. He turned to Prilly, who was now shocked by both the unexpected invitation and willingness with which this man would let her just leave. "Well, have a good evening," he said as he turned and started walking down the street.

Prilly watched as he and Melville went into a café only half a block down. She turned to walk in the other direction but as if in slow motion stopped mid-movement and turned back towards the café. She would hate herself if she didn't check this out. When she walked into the café Pete was sitting on a long red velvet couch. He smiled and said, "Well, you changed your mind."

"I thought I'd just come for a quick coffee."

"Great." With that he jumped up and got in line next to Melville, cutting in front of several people who didn't seem to mind.

Prilly placed her brown bag on the couch and sat on a wooden chair opposite where Pete had been sitting. "What'll ya have," he hollered. "Oh, a cappuccino. A non-fat cappuccino please."

Soon the two men joined Prilly. "Thank you," she said as Pete handed her a drink. "My name is Pete, and this is Melville, my editor," Pete said with a smirk as he plopped down on the couch.

"I'm Prilly. Prilly Greene." Turning to Melville who was sitting in the chair to her right, she then said, "You're an editor? Me too, that's so funny. I'm at WISE. What house are you with?"

Pete started laughing and said, "The house of Jacob."

Melville stuttered a bit and Prilly, not knowing what was so funny, turned to Pete. "Are you a writer?" she asked.

"Yes. Graphic novels mostly, but I do a little of everything."

Prilly was disproportionately impressed by him considering they had just met. He was very sexy, too sexy for her really, but he seemed interested. She loved his British accent though she was embarrassed by her own trite thinking. He immediately reminded her of the lead singer from the '80s band Ah Ha. She had always loved the video for their song "Take on Me" in which the singer is transformed into a cartoon illustration who falls in love with a plain-looking diner waitress. Every time she saw that video she wondered why they didn't get a more glamorous woman to play the love-interest, but she cherished the video because it gave her hope. That was exactly how she felt with Pete.

After talking about the book reading for quite a while (although clearly a bit full of himself, Pete was well read and Prilly was enamored), they decided to go out for dinner. Prilly said that she wanted to stop at her apartment first to drop off the bag with her shoes. She actually wanted to freshen up and throw a toothbrush and some makeup in her pocketbook just in case she didn't make it home that night. Although she had no intention of sleeping with him, this was the most exciting thing that had happened to Prilly in a long time and she wanted to be prepared for spontaneity. Suddenly worried that she just invited two total strangers into her apartment, she felt a mix of trepidation and exhilaration as she clumsily turned the key in the lock. "I'll just be a couple of minutes, feel free to look at those books," she said pointing to her bookshelf as she darted into her bedroom. She returned ten minutes later with a larger handbag and without the brown paper bag that had become a source of gags on the way to her apartment. "Are you ready to go?" she asked.

"I'm going to go home. I forgot that I promised my brother I'd watch a movie with him tonight," Melville said. "He already rented it."

"Oh, ok," Prilly responded, not knowing if it was true or if Pete had asked him to make himself scarce so they could be alone. Though she was hoping the latter was true, that thought also made her stomach knot. She had never been with someone so good-looking before.

The three walked out together and Melville headed left while Pete and Prilly headed right.

*

When Melville entered his apartment Jacob was sitting on the couch with three guys that Melville had seen there before but had never been introduced to. They were passing around a joint and listening to some god-awful reggae music. Melville walked over to the refrigerator and took out a small bottle of Orangina and a Tupperware with leftover macaroni with meat sauce that he had made a few days earlier. He popped the Tupperware into the microwave. The 90 second cooking time felt like forever as Melville awkwardly stood waiting for it to beep. "Hey, I thought you were hanging with Pete tonight. Did he ditch you?" Jacob hollered from the couch. Suddenly there were four sets of bloodshot eyes peering over at him. "He met a girl. Wanted to be alone with her. She's beautiful," Melville quietly said, embarrassed that in fact he had again been ditched. With that Jacob and his friends refocused on their joint and Melville took his dinner into his room where he ate while listening to a Stravinsky CD and thinking of Prilly.

*

"'Casey bombed into town with her daily organizer.' Ha! That's terrible," Pete said as his voice became higher and his laughter morphed into a cackle.

"Really? You think so? It's not Pulitzer material but I don't think it's so bad. You should have seen the guy. He looked, he looked like he was trying to pretend he wasn't shattered. He's already one of our authors; I felt really badly for him."

"You've got to be kidding. It's dreadful. That could be an example in a book about how *not* to write. Maybe you could use it for that," Pete said, again punctuating his suggestion with laughter.

Pete was getting close to hurting her feelings, and he was definitely arrogant, but she let it slide and just said, "Yeah, I guess it's pretty bad" (even though she still didn't understand why).

After a two hour dinner sitting at the bar of a pub that Pete recommended (where they had gone Dutch), Prilly was in Pete's apartment sharing a bottle of red wine they picked up on the way there (which Prilly had paid for because Pete suddenly became fascinated looking at plastic lighters when it was their turn at the register). Normally Prilly would have been put off by such a scruffy little apartment, but on that night she saw the simplicity differently. He was living like a real artist, she thought.

With only one chair in the apartment Pete invited her to sit on the bed. When she hesitated he said, "Don't worry, you don't have to sleep with me or anything," followed by a short burst of laughter which she was beginning to realize was a regular part of his communication. "Oh, I know," she said uncomfortably as she went to sit on the bed being careful not to spill her wine.

Wanting to quickly start up the conversation Prilly asked, "What have you written? You said something about graphic novels. I don't know much about that genre but would I know your work?"

"Oh no. No, you wouldn't know my work. I haven't been ready to publish. Haven't sent it out anywhere. But soon."

As an editor Prilly didn't know what to make of this. She dealt with writers every day who were desperate to publish, who wanted it more than anything else. "When you say you're not ready to publish, do you mean that you haven't completed a work or are you one of those perfectionists who wants to get it all just so before you hand it over? Because you'd be amazed how useful copyeditors can be."

"Well I'll put it to you this way, if I were a gardener I would have the most beautiful, unusual flowers in the most unexpected and glorious colors. Everywhere the eye darted it would be unimaginable wonder. However, I wouldn't remember to water them and they would all die." He started laughing. "Besides, Melville does my copyediting."

"Ah," Prilly said, choosing to ignore the warning the universe might be sending her. She also chose not to ask how he earned a living (days later he would tell her that he lived mainly off of an inheritance from his parents who had both died young of lung cancer although neither were smokers). Instead of making her wonder about his work ethic it just made her feel sad for him.

They moved on to childhood tales (he had stories about eating candy floss on Autumn days; she had no idea what candy floss was but it sounded wonderful), his days in college (he was a philosophy major who dropped out during his third year because there was nothing more to learn from the professors), his subsequent adventures in London (where he befriended many drug addicted counter-culture artists) and eventually his move to New York (for "the energy"). She briefly told him about how much she loved her career, but mostly she just listened. After a few hours of talking, listening to new wave music that Prilly couldn't believe she had never heard before, and, flipping through folders of Pete's work that appeared as totally fragmented bits and pieces of rambling sprinkled with something magical, she realized it was past midnight.

"I should probably go."

"Don't be silly, spend the night. We can go out for breakfast in the morning. There's a wonderful little diner nearby with a fabulous waitress; she has the most unusual face, you have to see it. Do you have plans tomorrow?"

Prilly did have tentative plans with her friend Yvonne, and she wasn't sure if she wanted to sleep with Pete yet, but she just said, "No, no plans."

"Settled. I have only the one bed so you'll have to sleep with me but don't worry, we can just sleep. I'll get you a T-shirt to wear."

Prilly went into the bathroom and put on the oversized Smiths T-shirt he had given her. She looked in the small, toothpaste splattered mirror above the sink and wondered what she was doing. She also thought about how glad she was that she had brought her toothbrush.

She timidly returned to the bed, and carefully crawled in. Pete smiled at her and said, "Good night," as he flipped off the light switch. She lay awake for hours pretending to sleep.

The next morning, she heard Pete wrestling around in bed. She slowly turned to him, conscious of her morning breath. He looked her in the eyes and softly said, "Good morning." Not wanting to breathe on him she looked down and whispered, "Good morning." She turned around, lying with her back to him. He put his hand on her shoulder and she moved closer to him. He slid his hand under her T-shirt and rubbed her breasts. Then he moved his hands down and gently pulled her panties off. He put his hand on her and started slowly motioning. He slid into her and they made love, never turning to each other, never kissing.

After blowing off her friend with a text message in order to spend the rest of the weekend with Pete, Prilly floated into her office Monday feeling exhilarated. Even though she knew Pete was probably not terribly successful, all she could think about was how sexy he was and how lucky she was to have met him. Filled with thoughts of seeing him that evening, and wearing her lucky bronze colored sling back heels, she barely noticed Janice pop into her doorway before having a chance to turn her computer on.

"It's 9:15. You're always here right at 8:00. I was concerned. A little bit longer and I would have called you just to make sure you were ok."

Considering they had almost no relationship whatsoever, she wondered why Janice was feigning this concern for her. That thought temporarily distracted her from wondering why Janice was keeping tabs on what time she got into the office.

"Oh, I had a late night. So I decided to come in a little later today," Prilly said, suddenly realizing it was none of Janice's business.

Too focused on her own agenda to recognize an opportunity to prod for more information, Janice simply asked, "Well, what do you think?"

With no idea what Janice was talking about, Prilly asked, "About what?"

This caused Janice to roll her eyes, flip her hair, and sigh all at once. Prilly was worried she might hurt herself. She plopped down into the chair facing Prilly and responded sharply, "About the memoir series."

"Oh, right. I'm so sorry Janice but I was really busy this weekend and I didn't have a chance to look over the materials. Can I get back to you later in the week?"

"Prilly, this is really an excellent opportunity. And it's time sensitive. We need to get moving on this."

"Time sensitive?" Prilly wondered to herself. It wasn't time sensitive. But she realized that Janice was fixated and would be relentless. If Prilly ultimately turned her down, Janice would be out to get her in ways that may no longer be so subtle. If she agreed to work with Janice she would probably end up suicidal. It was a tossup. Feeling invincible from the two orgasms she had the night before, Prilly decided that with her personal life taking this wonderful unexpected turn, it wouldn't be such a bad time to take on a new work challenge. Maybe the series would be a hit; memoirs were interesting. Best yet, Pete would be impressed.

"Well, I still want to review the materials in order to understand what kind of commitment we're talking about, and what the compensation will be, but I think it's a good idea and I'd like to do it with you."

"Great. This is a terrific opportunity for you. I mean I don't really have time for it either but I think it will really strengthen our line and help your career." As Prilly was contemplating this last remark, Janice stood up and smiled. "I'll let Stu know. Let's set up a meeting later this week to go over the details and draft our work plan." And with that Janice left her office, closing the door behind her. Prilly worried about what she had just gotten herself into.

*

That night, feeling good about cajoling Prilly into the memoir series, Janice arrived home at 7:45 pm., with a canvas bag of groceries hanging on one shoulder and her maroon leather laptop bag in her hand. She hurriedly entered her house as the grocery bag started slipping. From the kitchen she shouted, "Richard, are you home?" as she unpacked green grapes, sliced turkey, wheat rolls and three bottles of Pellegrino sparkling water. To break the silence she hollered, "Kyle, Kyle please come here." Nothing. "He's probably out with his friends again," she thought. After making a turkey sandwich with a slather of Miracle Whip, the one taste of her childhood in which she found comfort, she flung her canvass bag on the coat rack near the front door, grabbed the computer bag she had abandoned there and headed into the dining room, which somehow, over time, had become her office. Sitting alone at the end of a long rectangular dark mahogany table covered with stacks of manila folders and books, she took out her folder labeled "ideas for the memoir series" and started to work with the untouched sandwich beside her.

*

Janice Goldwyn prided herself on three things: her career, her family and her house. More accurately, she prided herself on the appearance of her career, the idea of her family and, well, while she truly loved her house, she always feared that she best not get too comfortable there. So she didn't.

Growing up Janice didn't have much. She lived on the outskirts of Detroit. Her father was a nasty drunk. Janice desperately wanted his approval; so she worked her absolute hardest in school and came bounding into the house where she found him half reclined in his old sky blue Lazy Boy, drinking a beer and watching the Family Feud. She gently tapped him on the shoulder (after learning not to jump right in front of him thus obstructing his view). He always ignored her. Unable to contain her enthusiasm she happily said, "Pop, Pop, guess what? I got an A on my geography test" or "Pop, Pop, guess what, Miss. Murphy hung my painting up in art class" or "Pop, Pop, I beat my obstacle course record in gym class, maybe I can be a Marine like you someday." To all of these her father had the same response: "Biiiig nothing. Scatter. Scatter you piss ant." Unlike Janice's younger sister Marge who always despised their father and didn't care what he thought, Janice never stopped trying. Day after day, year after year, this scene played itself out. During this time Janice came to resent her mother, Myra. Somehow she came to see their situation as her mother's fault. She thought her mother must be inadequate, weak, a loser. When she hung all of Janice's crayon drawings on their refrigerator Janice concluded that she was too easily impressed. After long days at a factory clear across town, four bus rides, two there and two back, cooking, cleaning, sewing and countless other acts of sheer survival, Myra inevitably had to face a pathetic drunk's lifeless eyes and the scorn-filled eyes of her daughter who looked at her as if it were she who was pathetic. A quiet devout Catholic who believed her duty to her family disavowed her of the perils of wants of her own, she took it. She took it all, without request or complaint.

Janice grew both very ambitious and very resentful. Fortunately all of her work trying to impress her father resulted in acceptances to seven high ranking colleges, all of which were conveniently located far away from Detroit. She found it impossible to make friends in college. She had two part-time jobs (she had a partial scholarship and took out student loans to pay for the rest). One job was as a research assistant (which meant errand-girl but she told her sister in weekly phone calls that it was, "important work that would be published") and the other was working at the check-in station at the school fitness center (a job where she watched the "spoiled bitches and dumb-ass jocks" hang out while she sat reading Proust or Dostoyevsky, always for a class, never for pleasure). When she wasn't working she was studying, often pulling all-nighters. One night, when she was passing out at her desk trying to get through Adam Smith's economic theory, she pulled a yellow post-it note off her pad and wrote, "I'll sleep when I'm dead." She stuck it to her desk and used it for motivation. Anything less than an A devastated her. This often prompted her to offer to rewrite papers and do extra credit assignments. If professors responded that "grades weren't everything" she instantly detested them. Her initial sweet tone darkened and she accused them of "low-balling" her. Her schedule wasn't the reason she didn't have friends though. She resented the other students so intently that she mistook the smallest politeness, often causing her to say something cutting and totally unwarranted. For example, when her roommate offered to loan her "anything in her closet" Janice wrongly assumed the roommate was insulting her wardrobe (which she felt self-conscious about since she couldn't afford expensive clothing). Thus she responded, "Thanks, but I think I'm smaller than you" (which she wasn't). Although she did have three lackluster lovers, she hadn't had one true relationship, nor one true friendship.

Building her career was on the top of her life to-do list. Like everything else, Janice had to work for it. Nothing came easily. She constantly felt that the glass-ceiling was preventing her from excelling. She thought she was overlooked for promotions in favor of lesser men. When women were promoted ahead of her it was because they had slept with someone or were being controlled by someone-- "handled" she would say. Of course what Janice failed to realize was that although she was legitimately quite skilled at her job, she rubbed people the wrong way. The only thing standing in Janice's way was Janice.

As a result of her prickly personality, Janice never became the great success she felt she deserved to be. She had been stuck as an acquisitions editor without hope of making publisher. Though she was eventually given the history line to build, she had to fight for each author, each contract, each new idea. And while it was more interesting to her personally, it was a lateral move. She was merely re-positioned. The truth was that despite what she told Prilly she had been trying to start a memoir line for nearly four years. When Stuart finally agreed he didn't want her involved with the project at all, he wanted to give it to someone else in-house. Janice had a fit, threatening to sue him for sexual harassment, and so he agreed to let her co-edit the line, committing only to a test series. He suggested Prilly because he knew she was able to work well with others which would balance out the "Janice factor." Janice agreed because after being Prilly's supervisor she had a firm handle on Prilly's weak spots. She also knew that Prilly would never mistakenly see them as partners, as equals.

Janice routinely boasted to her husband, Richard, that she was much more successful than she was. He knew it wasn't true, he saw her paycheck and once a year he attended the annual WISE holiday party where it was very clear that Janice was neither important nor liked. Richard was a highly successful investment banker. He and Janice had met at a bagel store when they were both waiting for a fresh batch of poppy seeds to come out. He was short, only 5'5 (she was two inches taller) and the little hair he had was dark and curly.

CHAPTER 3

Although not terribly attracted to her, he slept with her that night to scratch the itch. He figured, why not. Janice called him twice that week. He was still itchy so he took her out to Docks Seafood Grill for dinner and then back to his house for a quickie. On their third date, which he thought would probably be their last, they went to a movie and then back to his house where they slept together again. He didn't even get undressed. He just pulled her underwear off from under her dress and then pulled his pants down to his ankles and got on top. He kept his eyes shut so that he could fantasize about his dental hygienist, a fair skinned red head who rubbed his arm when the dentist drilled. Janice was fantasizing about one of the college football players she often checked into the fitness center. He always smiled at her, revealing his dimples. And he always smelled like cedar. Richard didn't return any of her calls after that night until three weeks had passed, when he received a message from her that she was a week late getting her period. Once a doctor confirmed that she was pregnant he asked her to have an abortion. She refused, stating Catholicism as her reason (though she had long ago deserted the idea of a God, all-loving or otherwise). Richard wasn't the kind of man who wanted to have a woman he wasn't married to as the mother of his child. This was not because he believed in "doing the right thing" as his aging mother urged, but rather because he was embarrassed by it and perceived it as a hassle. After a period of continued dating, during which they developed a mild friendship, they married at City Hall, with Marge as their only guest, when Janice was seven months pregnant with their only child, a son they named Kyle. He made her sign a prenuptial agreement in exchange for which she convinced him to buy her a 2.5 carat emerald cut Tiffany diamond. She told everyone that they eloped in Saint Martin. Janice and Richard hadn't had sex in over four years.

Kyle, now a high school senior, had been Janice's project for years. Desperate to turn him into "something" (he was fairly homely with unwieldy dark hair, a large nose, and oily skin) she schlepped him to museums, sporting events and ethnic food

34

restaurants. She made him take piano classes (though he had no interest or talent) and karate (though he was terribly uncoordinated). Although Richard was very wealthy (with serious family money in addition to a lucrative career), they sent Kyle to public school. This angered Janice but allowed her to tell anyone who would listen all about how important it was that people support the public school system. Always a quiet boy, in recent years Kyle had become much more withdrawn, spending a lot of time alone in his room or "out with friends." Initially Janice was concerned, but over time she came to accept it as a normal part of being a teenage boy. She was just glad he had friends. She was also too busy to pay much attention. Richard worked twelve hour days at the office, and then generally spent the remainder of his time, including weekends, locked in his home office, secretly watching televised golf.

Their house was magnificent. It was a split level brownstone apartment that Richard bought during the big 1990s boom, after a bidding war when the widow of an old cultural attaché finally agreed to sell. It had high ceilings and mahogany floors and was filled with stunning pieces of antique furniture (many of which were Richard's family heirlooms). Anyone would be jealous of a home like this. Janice truly loved it. She speculated that most of her equally fortunate neighbors barely noticed their own homes. But, each day, as she walked through the large sculpted double doors, she appreciated what she had, often catching herself wandering through the house, looking up, with her eyes following the Victorian moldings.

Janice loved being able to say she was married to an investment banker. She loved wearing her diamond ring, which she religiously Windexed once a week for maximum sparkle. She loved showing up at the Christmas party every year with Richard who, at her request, was always dressed in an Armani suit. And she loved showing off pictures of Kyle (she always made sure to have blurry pictures, because even she knew what he looked like) who, she bragged, was both musical and athletic. In short, Janice loved the appearance of the life she had pasted together and tried to suppress the relentless fear that it was all a house of cards.

*

The next few weeks were the most intense of Prilly's life. Every day she hurried to her apartment after work to freshen up and grab an overnight bag. Then she'd head out to meet Pete either at his place or a teahouse where he would often hang out. Some nights they picked up takeout Indian food and ate on Pete's bed, listening to music and talking about art and politics. Other nights they went to underground dance clubs where everyone seemed to know Pete; especially the women. He held her hand as they walked around; it was extraordinary. She found herself doing things she never thought she would do. The Saturday after they met they were browsing in a vintage clothing store in the Village when Pete insisted that she try on a pair of faux black leather pants. After resisting to no avail, she tried them on. "Well look at you. You're hot girrrl!" Prilly happily bought them. She wore them four nights later to a club where they danced until 3:00 am. listening to wonderful trip-hop music she had never before heard. At his suggestion Prilly had worn silver body glitter on her neck and arms. The next day at work when Janice was in her office babbling on about the potential author list for their series, Prilly had to muster up all of her strength not to blurt out, "I wore body glitter last night. Body glitter! Can you believe it?" Every night ended the same, with the most intimate lovemaking of Prilly's life. Pete always unflinchingly locked his eyes to hers, except when he entered from behind. She had never felt anything like it. Some nights she took a cab home at 4:00 am; others she slept at Pete's. It was always an inner struggle. Although there was nothing that made her happier then falling asleep and waking up with him (sometimes he spooned her and she thought her heart might break from the beauty), she was invariably late to work when she stayed there. Some days she was very late, too late. One day she didn't arrive until almost 10:15, which Janice immediately pointed out to her, out of concern of course. Prilly thought it was a small price to pay for the fullness she suddenly felt.

She also thought that after another week or so things would settle down more and she would be better able to manage everything.

She knew she was in love with him by the Thursday after they first met. They were lying in his bed in the morning, he was asleep and she was waiting for the alarm clock to beep. He had one of those alarm clocks that starts off with four quiet beeps and increases in volume at seven minute intervals. She was always worried that she wouldn't hear it and often woke herself up shortly before it went off. This of course contributed to her increasing exhaustion resulting from her new schedule; a schedule she knew full well couldn't be maintained. Pete slept for hours after she left, but she had to race to work and then race to meet Pete, who seemed to blossom after 10:00 pm. The dark moons under her eyes were getting more difficult to mask with concealer. On that morning, as she lay awake waiting for the alarm to beep, she kept thinking, "Just a few more minutes, just a few more minutes. Let me lie here with him for just a few more minutes. Don't make it end. " Lying on that old mattress was the most alive she had ever been. This was a big life.

Late one night a week later, lying back to back, Pete whispered, "I love you." It was so quiet she wondered if she had imagined it. She lay awake tightly holding onto the possibility. Two days later, when he said it again, once again as they were falling asleep after making love, she whispered "I love you, too."

*

Soon Prilly realized that she was working hard to keep Pete's interest. Naturally there was nearly endless effort to look good: leg shaving, bikini waxes, makeup application, makeup touchups, high heels and assembling "arty" outfits that looked effortless. All this was dwarfed in comparison to trying to be interesting, which was getting considerably harder. He was always saying clever and insightful things. For example, when they went to the Modigliani exhibit at the MOMA he explained why the eyes in Modigliani's paintings were so special. She would have missed that. She tried to contribute her own insights about the peculiar shapes of the bodies.

Apparently this was a "pedestrian" remark. Sometimes he was very impressed by her, particularly her quick observations about the use of language (most of which were ideas she had borrowed from her authors); she reveled in the affirmation. Other times he looked at her the way one looks at a dirty puppy that will have to be cleaned. She felt as though there was an elixir running through her veins, and she was going to do what she could to keep it flowing. It was a lot of work.

"Hey, Melville, over here," Pete shouted as Melville twice scanned the teahouse looking for him.

When Melville walked over he was greeted with, "Fuck man, are you blind?"

Melville sat down at the small table and took off his jacket, hanging it on the back of his chair.

"What have you been up to?" Melville asked. "Haven't seen you much lately."

"Aren't you going to order something?"

"No, I don't want anything. If I'm thirsty later I'll just use the water fountain."

"You can't just sit here if you're not going to order anything. You think these people," Pete said as he started pointing to the staff behind the espresso bar, "You think these people want you coming in here just to sit?"

Melville didn't say anything. He stood up and got in line. He returned a couple of minutes later with a single shot espresso. He didn't drink espresso but it was the cheapest thing on the menu and he couldn't afford anything else. When he returned to the table Pete was reading. He just sat there for a few minutes and then repeated, "What have you been up to? Haven't seen you much lately."

"Been writing. I've nearly got the carnival part just right. And I've been hanging out with that girl, Prilly. Remember the one we met at the Winterson reading?"

"Remember?" he quipped back in his head. He had hardly thought of anything else. "Yeah, she seemed nice."

"Yeah, I like her. She's in publishing you know. She's been spending most nights at my place. She's meeting me here in about an hour; you can hang and have a coffee with us if you want."

"Sure."

"Clyde's been calling me lately too. She broke up with that loser and is coming out of her latest bender so you know. Whatever."

CHAPTER 4

With that Pete started reading again. Mesmerized by this last remark, Melville took a small paperback novel out of his inside jacket pocket and pretended to read.

*

Prilly sat staring at her watch as she waited in Stuart's office. At first all she could think about was that she was supposed to meet Pete in twenty minutes. She was going to be late. She started tapping her pen against the legal pad on her lap. Then she started to wonder why Stuart had asked to see her before she left. Prilly knew she had been trimming her hours lately and started to get nervous. She wondered if she looked tired. Was she in trouble? Just as her palms started to sweat, Stuart walked in.

"Sorry to keep you waiting. Marcy cornered me in the mailroom, and you know how hard it is to get away from her."

"No problem. What's up?" Prilly said as a feeling of indigestion bubbled up.

"I wanted to know how it's going with Janice."

"Oh," Prilly said feeling relieved. "It's fine. Everything's going well. She's put a lot of thought into this idea; so I'm really just along for the ride." This wasn't entirely true. While Janice was relentless with emails, voicemails and unscheduled meetings at her discretion, she was also demanding that Prilly implement many of her ideas, in short leaving Prilly to do most of the grunt work. Nevertheless Prilly didn't want to start something. Her newfound bliss also made her feel badly for someone whom she now thought was so obviously miserable.

"That's good to hear. I bumped into Janice earlier, and she led me to believe that there might have been some friction; division of labor and so forth. I told her I was confident that it could be resolved."

"Oh," Prilly said, stunned. "I'm surprised to hear that."

"Oh I wouldn't give it too much thought. Janice is a bit of a workaholic. I think she holds everyone to her standards. I'm sure it'll be fine."

"I have been working hard Stu. I've just been swamped with everything and this series is taking up a lot of time."

"I know. I know. Don't worry; I just needed to check-in. Just wanted to let you know I'm here if needed."

As Prilly stood up and thanked Stu she again remembered that she was late to meet Pete. She had to hurry.

*

Standing at the opposite end of the dining room table from where his mother sat working Kyle quietly said, "I'm going out now."

"Ok, see you later," Janice softly replied without glancing up from her laptop.

Kyle grabbed his olive green backpack and left, walking two blocks before heading down into the subway. While waiting on the platform he took his red Ipod out of his bag and started listening to the Cocteau Twins live BBC sessions. A minute later he was sitting on the train in between two elderly women. He got off five stops later and walked with his earphones on up to street level where one of his friends was waiting for him.

"Hey."

"Hey."

*

Prilly, who usually arrived to everything 15 minutes early, was so late that she didn't make her usual stop at home before rushing to the teahouse. She had left a toothbrush and some clothes at Pete's place, and she had taken to shoving her cosmetic case in her workbag in case of such an emergency. Worried that she might look worn-down, she stopped in a Starbucks a block away from the teahouse where she was meeting Pete. After waiting in a long, slow line she went into the foul smelling one-person unisex bathroom and quickly retouched her makeup. She then raced to meet Pete.

"Hey girl," Pete shouted from a corner table.

"Oh great, Melville's here," Prilly thought as she made her way over trying to slide between cramped tables without knocking her large bag into anything. She thought that Melville's sunken drooping eyes made him look like a weirdo, and she also found him oddly quiet. Besides, she was in a bad mood and wanted to be alone with Pete.

"Hey," she said plopping down on a spare chair and dropping her bag on the floor. "Were you waiting long? I'm really sorry, I got held up at work. You wouldn't believe the crap I'm dealing with."

"All good. No worries. I've been reading a wonderful book," Pete replied.

"I'm beat. Would it be ok if we picked up some takeout and just ate at your place?"

"Yeah, sure," he said putting his jacket on. With that he and Prilly left, with Pete saying, "See ya later" to Melville.

*

"She's just so two-faced," Prilly said as she maneuvered some lo mein into her mouth.

"Here, let me show you; you're not holding them right," Pete said as he illustrated how to properly place one's fingers on chopsticks.

Embarrassed, Prilly tried to copy him but moments later resorted back to her own way of holding them.

"Well, is there any truth to it? Have you been pulling your weight?" Pete matter-of-factly asked as he knocked a container of spicy pea pods over onto the old towel that lay across the bed as a makeshift tablecloth.

Unable to control her frustration at what felt like the second betrayal of the day Prilly snapped back, "She's just a bitch. Don't you get it? I'm doing *most* of the work, not just a little, but most of it. And I never wanted to do this in the first place, she bullied me into it. And what the hell is that to say something to my boss when she hasn't said a word to me? She's obviously up to something."

"Well then you've got to confront her. Take the venom out of it." But before Pete could continue his phone rang. He leaned over and grabbed it off of the floor. "Hello." He then turned his back and lowered his voice. "Hey, this isn't a great time I'm eating with a friend. Where? What's the address? I'll try to make an appearance but no promises. Yeah. Ok, bye."

"Friend???" Prilly thought. "Am I just a friend?" she wondered, as the speed of her animosity built like a getaway car on a rollercoaster straight from a childhood nightmare. "Who was that?" she asked most curiously.

"A friend of mine, Clyde. She's having some issues, just broke up with some guy, blah blah blah. She wants to see me. She's going to a small gothic club downtown in a bit. She was hoping I'd make an appearance."

"Oh, well I thought we were gonna stay in tonight. I'm tired and I'm upset. I don't really feel like going to a club."

"How about this, why don't you stay here and relax, maybe read or go to sleep and I'll slip out for a couple of hours?" Pete asked.

Prilly didn't know what to say. She couldn't believe that he would leave her there alone. And who was this woman that he wanted to see more than he wanted to be with her? A woman to whom Prilly was just "a friend"? She felt like bursting into tears but didn't want to let him know how upset she was so she coldly said, "Well, I guess, if that's what you want to do. I can just go home."

"No, no, stay here. Stay, relax, listen to music, eat this food and I'll be back in a couple of hours."

With that Pete jumped up and walked to the bathroom, bringing the container of lo mein with him. Prilly just sat there. She heard the shower turn on. She heard it turn off. She heard the sink faucet turn on, then off. She heard him open the bathroom door. She mostly heard the angry voice in her head; a high pitched voice, which by this time wouldn't shut up. She just continued to sit there silently, fuming. All she had wanted all day was to be with Pete and now he was ditching her for some other woman. He came into the room and casually said, "Hey girl," and smiled, as if totally unaware of the angst he was causing her. He put the nearly empty Chinese food container down on the bed saying, "That's delicious. I couldn't stop myself," and laughing. As he bent over she could smell his newly spritzed cologne. She wanted desperately to remain silent; to stay cool. She had been telling herself over and over and over again during the 25 minutes he was in the bathroom that she needed to play it cool. But after that whiff of his cologne she blurted out, "Who is this friend? Is she an old girlfriend?"

He chuckled. "If you're asking if I've slept with her, yeah, sure. But we're friends. She's going through a bad time, and she wants to talk. I kind of feel like getting out tonight, and you don't. Even if you did, I don't think it would be the best time to introduce you. I broke up with her, and now she just broke up with someone, and you know."

No, Prilly didn't know. She didn't know why the man she was crazy about, the man she was running all over town to see though utterly exhausted was leaving her to see another woman whom he had slept with; who may still have feelings for him! She could feel rage brewing and feared it would slip out her lips. She held onto it as tightly as she could; worrying that she might induce a stroke.

He leaned down and kissed her on the forehead. As he bent over she heard his black leather pants squeak. They were tight, and with a long black and silver long sleeve T-shirt over them, he looked sexy. He smelled good, and he looked sexy. She was livid.

*

When Pete left with a, "See ya girl," as he shut the door, Prilly experienced physical paralysis and mental turrets. She couldn't stop wondering what had just happened. In her mind, over and over again, "What just happened?" Then she started to obsess about Clyde, this woman Pete was so eager to see. She knew he had slept with other women of course, and by his unmatched sexual talents she figured there had been many of them, but she didn't want to think about it; she didn't want to know about them. She mostly didn't want him to care about them. "Clyde, Clyde. She's probably really beautiful. She sounds beautiful. She's probably really cool. She probably wouldn't mind if he ran out to see an old girlfriend. She's probably beautiful." As she sat in his little apartment that now stunk of Chinese food, a smell she couldn't get rid of long after putting away the leftovers and washing the dishes, she thought she might be sick. The longer she waited, the angrier she got. "Who the fuck is he to leave me like this? What kind of fucking man does this? He doesn't care. He doesn't care about how I feel!" She decided to get ready for bed and lie there pretending to sleep until he got home. She wanted to look good, assuming they would make love after he apologized and told her how wonderful she was; so she brushed her teeth but slept with her makeup on. She didn't want to really fall asleep, afraid she would have bad breath and messy hair by the time he returned; so she just lay in bed thinking, spinning. Four and half hours passed with each minute experienced like the labored breaths of an old woman on her deathbed. She twice got up to rinse her mouth with Listerine and to powder her nose. She felt pathetic, really pathetic, and she knew she should just get up and leave, without a note or phone call. But she lay there, counting the seconds. Her thoughts vacillated from Pete to Clyde to Janice and Stuart. Suddenly her big life was shrinking.

After 2:30 am she heard a key in the door. Pete went straight into the bathroom and then, ten minutes later, made his way to the bed where she lay pretending to sleep and afraid he could hear her overpowering heartbeats. When he got into bed, she rustled around a bit so he would think he woke her up. He didn't say anything and she could feel his back to her, so eventually she just went to sleep. She woke up at 5:00 am in a cold sweat, and then fell back to sleep.

The next morning Prilly got up, showered and dressed and made two mugs off coffee with Pete's one-cup coffee maker. There was only a little cream left, and she used most of it in her coffee thinking "screw him" to herself. She stood in the kitchen, looking through the cut out wall, trying to read his mind as he lay sleeping. Was she overreacting to the night before? Was she being too sensitive? Did it mean anything? Why didn't they make love when he got home? She couldn't wait for him to wake up and somehow make it better.

After an hour and forty-five minutes of waiting, trying to subtly make just enough noise to wake him without being obvious, he finally woke up, rubbing his eyes and clearing his throat. "Hey. I smell coffee," he said in a low voice.

"Yeah, I made you a cup. You might have to nuke it, it's been sitting for a while."

"K. Thanks," he said as he stood up, wearing the same long sleeve T-shirt he had left in, now paired with his black boxers. He lifted his arms high into the air, and made a loud yawning noise as he stretched upward. "I have to go to the bathroom, I'll be right there."

The next two minutes seemed somehow to be a hundred times longer than all those that preceded them. Prilly stood in the kitchen, sipping her cold coffee, not knowing what to do. Pete came in and kissed her on the forehead, grabbed his coffee and then went to the refrigerator for cream. He spilled the last drops into his mug and said, "We're out of cream," to which she replied, "I know." He took his mug and walked past her into the bedroom. He propped his pillow up against the wall, and sat down on the bed, with his legs outstretched, drinking his coffee. Furious, Prilly made a loud sigh and walked into the bedroom with her mug in hand. She sat in the computer chair and just as Pete started to smile at her she said, "So, you got home late last night."

"Yeah, sorry. Once it was midnight I figured you were asleep and that it didn't matter so I stayed a bit longer. Didn't want to call and wake you."

In a sharp tone she responded, "Well, did you have a good time? Is your friend ok?"

"Oh, you know, she's always going through something. She has a tinsel heart you know. She's like a bird that you want to take care of."

"What the fuck is this?" Prilly screamed inside her head. "Doesn't he know how upset I am? Can't he see that I'm upset?" And then the silent anger quickly turned to hurt. "Tinsel heart? Bird? Is everything about her beautiful? It sounds like he loved her. Maybe he still loves her." Despite all of these thoughts swimming in her mind, she managed to stay silent. It took a lot of effort but the more special Clyde sounded, the less she wanted to reveal how very not-ok she was with all of this.

"The club was cool. You would like it; we should go sometime. It was very small, dark, and the walls were covered with dark purple fabric, like a flowing translucent kind of fabric. The music was wonderful, a terrific Deejay; lots of trippy stuff like Portishead. I danced a lot."

Fighting every inclination she had, she remained quiet, just looking at him, silently screaming, "What the hell is wrong with you?"

"I'm gonna hop in the shower. Starving. You want to go to that diner again, the one with the fabulous waitress?"

"Sure," she said feeling relieved that they were spending the day together but also angry and utterly confused.

With that Pete got up and went to the bathroom to shower.

*

An hour later they were sitting in the diner, waiting for someone to take their order. "I'm ravenous; feel like I could eat a horse," Pete said, seeming particularly jolly this morning, Prilly thought.

"Hmmm. So you said."

The waitress walked over, and Pete smirked at Prilly; it was not the waitress with the wonderful face. This much younger waitress had a very long, thin face with long, thin features and elfin ears.

"She's a bit bird-like," Prilly thought. "Not a pretty bird, but a bird." She looked at the nametag on her canary-colored uniform: "Ruth". "Clyde is probably a beautiful bird," Prilly imagined.

"I think I'll try an omelet today," Pete said, as if the waitress knew his regular order, or cared, "With mushrooms and cheese, cheddar cheese."

"What kind of toast?

"Wheat. With marmalade, not jam."

"And for you?"

"Oh, um, I'll have the blueberry pancakes please."

"Shit," Prilly thought to herself. "What am doing? First the lo mein last night and now pancakes. I'll have to suck my stomach in all day."

"So what do you want to do today? There's a Shepard Fairey exhibit at the Guggenheim I'm dying to see. Do you know his work?"

"No."

"Oooh, he's wonderful. He's famous for that Obama poster you know, but his other work, his real work is marvelous. It's all very subversive, like the guerrilla art I told you my friends in London were into. There's a marriage between word and image in the work. Very carefully done. Sharp and sardonic. And the Guggenheim, well fuck, that building is an orgasm itself."

"Uh, huh," Prilly said, totally unable to focus on anything he was saying.

She then blurted out, "What happened last night? I mean, you totally ditched me and went out with some woman you've slept with before and then you don't come home til the middle of the night. Do you know how that makes me feel?" As soon as the words came out she felt regretful for saying them and desperate to hear his response.

He laughed. He laughed and then with a close-mouthed smile he managed to make her feel even more pathetic than she already did. "It was nothing. A friend called me and she needed me. You could have come but you weren't up for it last night. You know how I feel about you. What we have is what we have, it has nothing to do with Clyde or with anyone; so it shouldn't matter whether I've slept with her or not."

"Well you might not feel that way if it was you."

"If it were the other way around I wouldn't care. I know what we have, and I wouldn't worry, and I wouldn't want to stop you from doing something you wanted to do."

Unsatisfied, Prilly asked, "Were you, were you in love with her?"

"Love, I don't even know what love is. Love is just a word people say to each other. I care about her, sure."

"Love is just a word people say to each other? He doesn't even know what love is? What the fuck is he saying? How can he say this when he said he loved me? He said it first. And he said it twice. How can he be saying this?" Prilly wondered. What she actually said out loud was, "I felt like you abandoned me. I was really upset, you knew I had a bad day at work, and we made plans and then you just left. And what's worse, you left to see some woman you had a relationship with. How did you think that would make me feel?"

And with that Ruth brought the food over. Pete said "thank you" and started eating immediately, sprinkling salt on his omelet with one hand as he ate a forkful of home fries with the other. Prilly just sat there, staring at him.

A few moments later he put his fork down and said, "Look, I'm sorry if you were upset. Honestly, I didn't think it was a big deal. I thought you were cool with it."

"Ok, I guess we can just drop it," Prilly responded, not quite sure if she had blown it all into something bigger than it was, but certain she didn't want things to escalate further. She cut up her pancakes, drizzled on some syrup and started to eat, trying to convince herself she wasn't really as upset as she was. After a few bites Pete said, "You know, I don't believe in the traditional monogamy thing. I mean, I thought we were cool, that we had an unspoken understanding, but maybe it's best to lay our cards on the table."

Unable to take in the oxygen necessary in order to comprehend this information or formulate a response, Prilly sat silently for a moment. Before she could speak Pete continued on, "I mean, we're having a wonderful time, and it's very special; so there's no reason to label it. What a person has with one person doesn't take away from what they have with someone else. Like with Clyde. What I had with her doesn't take away from how I feel about you. It's totally different."

"Too many thoughts, too many thoughts to process," Prilly frantically thought to herself as she took another bite of blueberry pancake in order to buy enough time to steady her voice. "I don't understand. We've spent every day together since we met." And then leaning in and lowering her voice she said, "You told me you love me."

He again smiled, close-mouthed. "I said what was in my heart in the moment. I always do. And it is always true. This you can count on. So who needs false promises when you have that?"

She thought to herself that maybe this Clyde woman, who ever she was (and she did sound wonderful) could see the beauty in what Pete was saying; she probably could, "tinsel heart" and all, but to Prilly it just felt hurtful; very, very hurtful. She wondered if they had been in the same relationship at all. She felt foolish.

"I still don't understand. Are you saying that you're seeing other people or that you want to? Did something happen with Clyde last night? Is that why you came back so late?"

He offered up another close-mouthed smile and then, "No, no, nothing happened with Clyde if that's what this is really about. But even if it had, it wouldn't need to change anything we have. Clyde was once a special person in my life, and she is still sort of in my life but I haven't slept with her since we broke up before I met you. I think she wanted to last night. She was very vulnerable. But truthfully all I could think about was you at my place, in my bed, waiting for me. I thought it was sweet how you let me go, how you knew it was ok."

"Again, too many thoughts; too many thoughts to process at once," Prilly thought, feeling overloaded. There was a lot of information and she feared none of it was good. She wanted to be cool. She wanted to be the sweet cool tinsel hearted girl who waited in his bed, but she wasn't. So she responded sharply, "It would matter to me."

"Look, two people can be together forever and be only with each other, but not because of some artificial promise. I don't believe in that. Sure, you can find a thousand men to be with who will give you hollow promises, but not me. That's not what I'm giving you. You have to live moment to moment. And the moments string together. And eventually you can string together a lifetime. But not because of promises, just because it is true to your heart, to your soul. You cannot cage a bird as they say."

"Great, more birds," Prilly thought as she said, "It wouldn't be all right with me if you were with someone else. That's not what I want."

He smiled again, letting out the quietest of laughs as if she were too provincial to understand what he was saying-- or too insecure to deal with it, the latter of which may well have been true.

"Ok, I understand. If anything were to ever happen with someone else, or if I wanted it to, I would tell you. You have my word. I would be honest with you and you could do as you needed to."

"Ok," Prilly softly said, not knowing how to make this dreadful conversation end in a way that would have them both sitting there-- and ideally in a way that would restore the feeling to her numb feet.

"But I don't want to be with anyone else right now. I like being with you," he said, as if he were giving her a gift. Just as she had so many times in earlier years, she felt like Charley Brown dumping out a Christmas stocking full of coal.

*

On the way to the Guggenheim Pete wanted to "dash into Starbucks for a dopio espresso." He said he was still feeling "wiped and the diner coffee sucked." When he and Prilly hurried in she noticed Melville sitting by the window. This time she was glad to see him. "I'll just have a bottle of water please," she said to Pete as she plopped down next to Melville. Pete put his hand out. Embarrassed on every level Prilly reached into her bag scrambling for her wallet. She pulled out a five and handed it to him. "Do you want anything?" she asked Melville. Not accustomed to being offered anything he just shook his head. "So, what's up?" she asked.

"Um, nothing really. Just reading a book," Melville shyly replied.

Prilly grabbed the book from him. "Wow, this looks good. I love novels set in Victorian times." With this, she glanced over to spot Pete whooping it up with the pretty young barista behind the counter. Suddenly she was replaying their relationship in her head. She had thought these had been the best weeks of her life but now, as she rewound, all that she could picture were all of the times he had flirted with waitresses, made small talk with female bartenders or spoken to strange women in cafes after she had hurried from work to meet him. Feeling terribly insecure and in need of affirmation she looked at Melville, who she had an inkling might like her, and said, "You know Melville, I met you when I met Pete. Remember? Did you ever think it might be different? That it could have been different that day, and you and I might have ended up together?"

With a stone face concealing his astonishment he stuttered a bit and said, "Well you and Pete seem to make a good couple," while he secretly thought, "Yes, yes, I think about it all the time, and I hate myself for not having been able to talk to you first; knowing it never would have been me."

Totally distracted by his last "couple" comment, she was markedly unaware of the effect she was having on Melville, who felt increasingly tortured. She slumped down balancing her elbows on the table and putting her head in her hands, muttered, "Yeah, well, couple. What's a couple, right?"

Melville was too caught up in his own thoughts to realize how incoherent she was. Like most people, Prilly was speaking to a tape in her head that no one else could here. "Hey Melville, do you know Clyde?"

"Yeah, sure."

Prilly leaned in closer, "She and Pete were a thing right?"

"Yeah, I thought they were the real thing."

As Melville's heart raced at the smell of Prilly's apple-blossom shampoo, Prilly's heart sank at confirmation of her worst fear: Pete had been in love with Clyde.

Suddenly Prilly heard Pete say "thanks Hon" to the barista in his ever-sexy voice and she leaned back as he made his way over. When Pete returned he handed Prilly the bottled water-- without change, she noticed-- and remarked, "You know the plastic in these things is probably worse than the tap water. Ha. And all these supposedly environmentally conscious people drink these but what do they think all of these plastic bottles do to the environment? That's an inconvenient truth," Pete said through intermittent laughter.

Prilly was in no mood to be criticized. She was sitting there heartbroken and he was lecturing her about her beverage choice.

"Ready to go," he said, oblivious as ever Prilly thought.

"Sure. Why doesn't Melville come along?" Prilly suggested, surprising them both.

After a brief pause Melville said, "Oh, no it's ok."

"No, come on. We're going to the Guggenheim to see some art exhibit Pete's all excited about. Come with us. It'll be fun."

"Come with us; don't just sit here all day," Pete said. Somehow even his invitation made Melville sound feeble.

"Ok."

And with that, the three left making their way on foot to the Guggenheim.

CHAPTER 5

Janice had a very particular weekend routine. Every Saturday she woke up bright and early to find her husband was already out. She invariably thought that he must be at the squash club; which was his weekend morning ritual. She hurried out of bed with great urgency to discover her family was nowhere to be found. (Kyle was either sleeping or out; she assumed he left early in the morning but never quite knew for sure if he had ever returned the night before). It never registered that surely they would be nowhere to be found, so she rather pondered to herself about where in the house they might possibly be. Then she raced to the kitchen, where standing in her long tangerine kimono purchased when "Asian styles" were in, she made a pot of decaffeinated coffee. She always bought whatever brand was on sale, normally some sort of dry roasted Colombian blend in a large canister covered with dust. She emptied the dishwasher as the coffee dripped. Then she poured some into her Cornell College mug adding only one Splenda, and trotted off to her bedroom to make the bed complete with military corners. She then went to her makeshift office in the dining room and checked her email and read her favorite blog, a humorous pop feminist blog by a Canadian writer from whom she stole many ideas. Next she decided to "do a little work." This decision typically caused her to work for several hours, getting up occasionally to refill her coffee or grab a bunch of grapes. Typically she didn't have work that required her to work these extended hours; so she simply obsessed about the work that she did have, often coming up with piles of "new ideas" that Stu later rejected. She also enjoyed creating lists of "things to do" for her various projects, followed by lists of what can be outsourced (these days mostly to Prilly). By late morning she needed to "clear her head" which she accomplished by riding her stationery bicycle in the windowless guest room across from her second floor bedroom. Sometimes she watched public television on the small old TV in the room. Then she showered and got ready for the day. Next, lunch. Typically this consisted of a sandwich of some kind, which she ate at the dining room table and which invariably caused her to "do a little more work while she's sitting there." By late afternoon Kyle made an appearance. Although he often went into the dining room to chat with her, by then she was always deeply engrossed in the unnecessary work she was doing. She wouldn't look up, and so Kyle would leave. By around 5:30, with the day gone, and no longer able to stare at her computer screen, she often wandered around her house until it was time to go out with her husband. They usually had a work-related dinner with his colleagues. She always did her best to make conversation but found it tiresome. She often complained to Richard's colleagues that she was so overloaded with work she had to, "Again work all day. Can you believe it? I don't know when I've had a day off." Sensing his colleagues felt badly for her, she felt free to talk even more about the demands of publishing "at her level." She always thought these dinners went very well considering how stressed she was. Nights when there was no business obligation, they sometimes went out to dinner alone making small talk about "getting the car checked" and such. Other nights Janice just spent the evening by herself, usually eating takeout in bed while watching television. Sundays were almost exactly the same except she called her sister and they never went out to dinner.

By the time she got to work on Mondays she was angry that she had been so swamped with work that she could not enjoy her weekend. Accordingly, she was often difficult to deal with, particularly to those who made the mistake of telling her about how they had spent their weekend.

There were only two exceptions to this weekend routine. First, twice a year Janice and Richard took a vacation. Every Spring they spent one week in Phoenix visiting Richard's sister Vicki and brother-in-law James. Janice and Vicki usually spent afternoons together going to local craft markets. Janice always bought some silver and turquoise jewelry crafted by Native Americans. She haggled about the price well past the point of acceptability by anyone else's standards. Vicki was always mortified but never said anything, since it was the only time all year she "had" to see Janice. Then over lunch Janice would go on and on about how she liked to "buy the local crafts to support the Native Americans." Desperate for an anesthetic Vicki usually ordered a glass of white wine with her lunch saying that it was a "special occasion; a girl's day."

Richard and James spent mornings at a local health club. James hated playing squash with Richard. Richard took it way too seriously and would have James running around the court the whole time. They would then return to the house where Richard excused himself to work. Not only did he bring his laptop, Blackberry and blue tooth, but he scheduled lengthy conference calls. Late in the afternoon Vicki would say she was a bit tired from the wine at lunch and she would excuse herself for a nap. She usually lay on her bed watching the travel channel on mute. Janice sat outside on their wrap-around porch admiring the exquisite scenery. The dramatic landscape composed of shades of burnt amber impressed her. Before marrying Richard she had never seen anything like it. After half an hour on the porch she invariably ended up at their dining room table, with her laptop, working. In the evenings they all went out to dinner. When Kyle and his cousin Natashya were younger they were there too-- requiring parental attention so that there was little need for the adults to come up with topics of conversation. Since Natashya went to college to study film at NYU two years earlier, Kyle refused to go on the trips. This allowed them to talk about their kids when they had exhausted such topics as "how wonderful dinner is" and "how great it is to take some time off to be together." Vicki secretly harbored anger towards Janice and Richard for not extending themselves more to Natashya while she was living in New York. They had invited her over for dinner only once (Chinese takeout) and taken her to one Broadway show (*Wicked*) in the two years she was living in the city. James didn't know why Vicki found that so offensive.

On their other annual trip Janice and Richard went to an exotic Caribbean island for a week. They stayed at a five star resort. Janice loved being waited on by the staff. When they stayed at the Four Seasons in Nevis the cabana boys walked around on the beach spraying guests with Evian water. Janice couldn't get enough of it; although she also felt that she had snuck into a member's only club and might get caught at any moment. To compensate she was overly demanding of the staff; to make sure they knew she belonged there. This was the only time all year when Janice and Richard really spent time together. Mostly they lied on the beach on lounge chairs each reading their own book. Richard often worked on his laptop in the evenings after dinner, and Janice went to sleep alone. When she returned from these trips she boasted about her fabulous vacation for weeks to anyone in the office she could corner long enough to listen.

The other exception to her weekend routine was when she met one of her girlfriends for lunch, sometimes followed by shopping or a museum visit. She only had three friends with whom she spent time by herself. And although she enjoyed an occasional lunch during which they caught up on work, kids and so forth, she never created any real intimacy, and the conversation, at least on her end, always remained at the surface level. She liked having friends though who complained to her about their problems-- and to whom she could complain about how hard she was forced to work and how undervalued she was. These conversations made her feel good about herself.

On this particular Saturday she had lunch plans with her friend Sarah Cohen, a feminist historian she met at a WISE event years ago. As usual, she had woken up bright and early that morning to discover Richard was already out. "He's probably playing squash at the club," she thought to herself. After making her decaf coffee and checking her email she decided to jump on the exercise bike for an hour and then get ready to meet Sarah. As she selected her outfit, choosing her favorite charcoal gray pencil skirt paired with a thin black V-neck sweater, she started to regret making plans with Sarah. She wasn't in the mood to hear about her boyfriend (a public school teacher whom Janice had met once at a book party), and Sarah had a way of being particularly draining. As she unrolled her black tights up one leg at a time she thought about how Sarah would go on and on, and Janice wished she could stay at home to get some work done.

Janice always arrived everywhere early. When she went out on weekends she carried the streamline black Prada pocketbook Richard had given her for Christmas two years earlier (he always gave her a "statement piece" on Christmas, her birthday and their anniversary, and she adored them). She was able to slide one manila folder of work into the thin rectangular bag. She felt less self-conscious waiting for someone if she had a project to occupy her. It also sent a message to the person who in Janice's mind was late, thus squandering her time (late to Janice was anything after she had already arrived; although she routinely arrived fifteen minutes early, making it nearly impossible for any normal person not to be "late"). Although trying to feign interest in the folder of "memoir series notes" she was looking at, Janice noticed Sarah immediately when Sarah arrived at the restaurant at noon (Janice naturally clocked her in at fifteen minutes late). It was hard not to notice Sarah. An ex-hippy, she wore long flowing Indian-inspired multi-colored skirts with tank tops adorned with many long layers of ornate chains or large beads. On this day, Sarah was wearing a long merlot colored skirt with a black pattern of some indiscernible kind, a white tank top and four multi-length necklaces of silver coins that sounded like wind chimes every time she moved. Sarah was petite and very pretty, with waist length nearly black hair in natural spiral curls. Janice thought Sarah would be beautiful if she dressed in more sophisticated clothing and tamed her hair although paradoxically she admired her for having her own unique style. Janice always experienced some dread before seeing Sarah; however, as soon as she did see her she remembered the many things she liked about her. On this day the always effervescent Sarah couldn't stop talking.

"Oh, there's my friend," Sarah hollered as she floated past the hostess, who pointed to the far corner where Janice had taken the booth seat. "Hi, hi, hi. Oh, don't get up," she said as she plopped down on the chair across from Janice, throwing her large canvass tote on the chair beside her. "Hope I didn't keep you waiting. I'm starving."

"Oh, no, it's fine. I was just catching up on some work."

"Busy?" Sarah asked as she started reading the menu.

Janice sighed and gently moved a strand of hair that was aggravating her eye. "I'm swamped. I'm telling you, you can't even imagine."

"I hope they appreciate you over there."

"Ha. You can't imagine. It's a real mess there. I work more than anyone and they don't like it. They're threatened by me. I'm a big producer, and it makes others look bad; so they try to marginalize me as much as they can. No one's doing me any favors. That's for sure. If I wasn't committed to my authors, I'll tell you, I wouldn't bother."

"That's awful. There's so much of a bias against women too. I bet if you were a man they'd be in awe of you, but because you're a woman they're threatened."

"Absolutely," Janice said as she nodded while thinking to herself that sometimes Sarah was really spot-on.

"Well, have I got a story for you. It'll take your mind off of your work," Sarah said as the waiter came over and asked if they wanted to order a drink.

"Actually I think we're ready to order lunch," Janice responded. Sarah nodded as she scoured the menu. "I'll have a club soda with lime and the chicken tortilla salad," Janice said.

"And for you Miss?" the waiter asked unable to stop staring at Sarah.

"An ice tea, unsweetened and the beet salad without cheese. Thanks."

"Very good."

"I stopped eating dairy a month ago, and I feel terrific," Sarah told Janice, as if to explain her order.

"What do they call that? Vegan?" Janice asked.

"Yeah, now I'm a full-fledged vegan. I read an op-ed in the *New York Times* that reported reducing meat intake by 20% is the equivalent of going from driving a Toyota Camry to driving a Prius. Can you believe it? So I figured since I didn't miss meat when I gave that up I would try the non-dairy thing too. It's been terrific. I'm full of energy."

"Uh huh," Janice said, suddenly thinking Sarah sounded stupid.

"So, you're not going to believe this. Remember that Israeli-Palestinian peace group I'm in?"

Janice said "yes" even though she couldn't remember. Sarah was always hung up on some new cause or joining some new group, none of which interested Janice, so she didn't keep track.

"Well, we had lined up a panel of speakers to coincide with the New York City Human Rights Festival. Remember I forwarded you that email?"

Janice nodded.

"Anyway, I somehow volunteered for the party planning committee for the opening reception. Just a low-key social event; wine and appetizers kind of thing. We had like no budget; so there's only so much you can do. Someone suggested doing the food potluck style which I thought was a great idea. Save money, get the people on the committee involved, easy for me."

"Uh huh," Janice said, looking intently at Sarah despite that she had already bored of the story.

"Well, days before the reception I get a call from Joanne who is also on the planning committee-- and kind of the main defacto organizer of our group. Apparently a couple of Kosher people who aren't in our group but wanted to come to the event requested that only Kosher food be served. Joanne told them that wasn't going to be possible since arrangements had already been made but that they were welcome to contribute Kosher dishes to the buffet."

"Uh huh. Did that satisfy them?" Janice asked, trying to show that she was paying attention.

"Nope. Not at all. They said that it would not be acceptable to serve non-Kosher food at this kind of event. I'll spare you every detail but suffice it to say Joanne wanted to get this person off the phone; so she told him to call me. I talked to the guy and got a long education about what it means to prepare and serve a Kosher buffet and that simply adding a Kosher-made dish would not suffice. I told him we had no intention of serving shrimp wrapped in bacon but that we had some Palestinian committee members who were planning on serving hummus and other salads. I thought that maybe dishes that didn't contain meat might be ok."

"And?" Janice asked, totally missing Sarah's humor regarding the bacon-wrapped shrimp.

"He said that he understood but wouldn't be able to attend. So after a year and a half of volunteering with this peace process group I couldn't even get people to agree on a politically and culturally acceptable buffet! How do you like that?!?"

Janice smiled. "Religion is a tough thing to battle with. People are very sensitive about it," she said in a serious tone that was incongruous with Sarah's zealous storytelling.

"Doesn't give me much hope for world peace," Sarah said, now unable to control her laughter. With that, the waiter returned with their salads, and they ate lunch.

Sarah was meeting her boyfriend that afternoon to see a series of documentary shorts at a nearby independent movie theater. She invited Janice who insisted she needed to get some more work done. They hugged at the door of the restaurant and parted ways. It was such a beautiful crisp day that Janice decided to walk home. On the way she stopped at a corner grocer. She looked at the flowers extensively but hated spending money on something fleeting. She ended up picking up some pink lady apples and a bottle of cranberry juice and headed home.

*

That night Meville approached his apartment with dread. He could hear hip hop music blaring from the downstairs corridor and knew Jacob was probably having another awful party. When he opened the apartment door a wave of smoke assaulted him. He started coughing as he made his way through the small darkened living room lined wall to wall with people he had never seen. No one seemed to notice him as he went straight to his room. He flung his jacket on his chair, staring longingly at the Mozart CD case on his desk. He lay on his couch with his hands behind his head. He thought he could see his room vibrating with each blast of reverberated noise. Eventually he shut his eyes. He wanted to masturbate but was scared someone would walk in so he pulled his blanket up to his chest, unzipped his pants and did it quickly.

*

As they arrived back at Pete's apartment Prilly felt increasingly anxious. All she could think about was Pete leaving the night before, Clyde—a stranger whom she suddenly couldn't stop wondering about, and worst of all, those awful words at the diner: "love is just a word... I don't even know what love is... I don't believe in promises... I will tell you if I want to be with someone else." Over and over she kept replaying these words and Melville's remark that Pete and Clyde "were the real thing" in a muddled mess interspersed with images of Pete intently looking at her while they made love and how she felt so alive she could see sounds and hear colors.

She mindlessly followed Pete into the apartment. He was still talking about the Fairey exhibit.

"The consumerism stuff is a bit pedestrian but good anyway. I mean, I've seen more inventive stuff. The whole church-state thing has been done. But you gotta hand it to him, the collection as a whole makes a statement."

"Uh huh."

"There was also some filler though. The portraits of the musicians are fun but disconnected from the larger work. I mean yeah, they're all resistive counter-culture artists but they're not political in the ways he's suggesting. I mean I get the subversive artist thing, but it didn't all hang together like the other work. I would have done it differently."

"Uh huh. Yeah, I liked those pieces though. Music gets at people in its own way," Prilly said as she plopped down on the edge of the bed, tossing her bag on the ground.

"Hey you," Pete said in his sexiest voice as he glanced over through the cut-out wall from the kitchen where he was guzzling a canned energy drink.

She smiled at him.

As he made his way over to her she couldn't quiet her mind. "What's going on? What is this? What am I doing here? How does he feel about me? Why does he look at me that way if he doesn't love me? Why? How could he want to be with someone else when I can only think of him?"

With one touch of his hand to her shoulder, her thoughts scampered and she looked up at him, hoping for a sign. As they made love her eyes locked onto him. She kept thinking, "He will see what I am trying to show him; he will see what I feel and he will tell me he feels the same; I know he does."

Afterwards she lay in his arms waiting, making a conscious effort not to fall asleep. If he held her long enough, after that beautiful intimate love making, he would give his whole self to her, as she thought he once did.

"You're beautiful."

She smiled softly as she looked up into his eyes.

"Are you hungry? I'm starving. I think I have some pasta. I could make a little spicy tomato sauce; I think I have some olives and capers. Want to help?" he asked as he sat up and grabbed his boxers from the floor beside him.

"Sure, that sounds good," she said as she leaned upward. Prilly got dressed as Pete headed to the kitchen.

They fell asleep two hours later after a pasta and red wine dinner eaten in bed followed by Pete reading more pages from his latest work. Prilly thought she was happy, but that night she woke up three times in a cold sweat. The last time she woke up Pete was holding her as he slept.

When she woke up in the morning she was surprised to find Pete already out of bed. "Hey girrrl. You're a sleepy head. I made you some coffee."

"What time is it?" she asked rubbing the corners of her eyes.

"It's only 10:30. I woke up feeling inspired this morning and had to get some stuff down. Funny how the brain works. That stuff we saw yesterday gave me some new ideas."

"That's great," Prilly said as she sat up and reached over the side of the bed searching for her underwear.

"I've been on to the word-image thing for years, I mean that's the whole graphic novel game when it's done right, but the way Fairey has whittled it down to literally marry the singular word and image, it's clever."

"Uh huh," Prilly said as she realized she was putting her tank top on backwards. Pete was still talking as she went to the bathroom to brush her teeth. She usually got up first expressly so she could freshen up before he woke up. When she came out he said, "come see this," as he motioned over to her from in front of his computer.

"Sure, let me grab my coffee," she said sleepily.

With her coffee in hand she walked over and stood next to Pete who put his right arm around her while he pointed to the screen with his left. She scanned the words in front of her while sipping her coffee. "I like it. It's ironic right?"

"Yeah. It's supposed to be humorous. But notice how I do that without diminishing the message."

"Yeah, it's good. I…" but before Prilly could say anything else the phone rang and Pete jumped up saying, "Hang on Babe, hold that thought."

As Pete answered the phone Prilly sat down in front of the computer and started scrolling down.

"Hey, it's not a good time. Yeah, sure. Will do. Bye."

"So girl, tell me what you think," he said as he made his way back over to her.

"Who was that?"

"Clyde," he nonchalantly replied.

"Oh."

"I told her I'd call her back," he said as he kissed the top of Prilly's head. "I know how it bothers you so I can wait and talk to her later after you've left."

"So basically you're saying that you'll just talk to her behind my back?" Prilly shouted as she leapt up knocking Pete back.

"What the hell?"

As Prilly hurried across the room and knelt to the floor where her clothes lay strewn she continued on, "You just don't get it. You don't understand how I feel. You don't care." She started frantically picking up her things and jamming them into her overnight bag.

"What are you talking about?" Pete said, now sounding annoyed. "Of course I care about your feelings. That's why I didn't talk to her now. I wanted to avoid this melodrama. It's not behind your back. I haven't lied to you," his voice rapidly elevating.

Putting her shoes on as quickly as possible she shouted, "You don't get it. You don't fucking get it," and she jumped up with her bag in hand.

"Fuck you. I don't need this shit. I haven't done anything wrong. You're crazy," Pete hollered. And with that Prilly stormed out slamming the door so loudly Pete was afraid it would come unhinged like she had.

*

Prilly opened the door to her apartment with her shoulders slumped, feeling physically unable to take another step. On the way home her rage had given way to a heaviness she had never felt before. She dropped her bag by the door and went straight into her bedroom. She took off her shoes, got into bed and pulled the covers over her head. She shut her eyes and begged God to let her fall asleep. When she woke up a couple of hours later she started crying and couldn't stop. After several hours like this she got up, put her robe on over her clothes and went to the kitchen. She put an emergency frozen fish sticks dinner in the microwave and opened a bottle of wine. Feet dragging, she brought her meal into the living room where she picked at it while watching two Lifetime movies starring Valerie Bertinelli. The second movie was based on a true story of a mentally ill woman who in a brutal conclusion stormed an elementary school with a gun and randomly shot a child. In an earlier scene that Prilly would never forget, the increasingly fragile woman kept buying raw meat at the grocery store and filling her otherwise empty refrigerator with it-- so much so that the meat started to spill out into her apartment. It was insane. Prilly wondered why the woman did that. She wondered if it made her feel better. Then she imagined the feeling of her hand penetrating a lump of ground meat.

*

That day Janice's phone rang at 2:30 in the afternoon. The ringing was a jarring interruption to the usual stillness. She got up from her dining room table where she was checking her email and walked into the kitchen to answer the phone. Upon picking up the wall phone she said: "Hello."

"Hey sis, it's me."

Surprised because they had already had their weekly call several hours earlier Janice stumbled a bit before saying, "Oh, hi. What's up? Did you forget something?"

"Something happened. Something bad."

Janice leaned against the wall and lowered her voice, "What is it Marge? What happened?"

"Dad was hit by a car. It's bad."

Janice stood against the wall, breathing slowly and trying to process what Marge had said. "How bad? Where is he?" she asked.

"He's at Mercy. He's in critical condition Jan. We don't know if he'll make it. They don't know the extent of his injuries yet. His legs were mangled. If he survives he may not be able to walk. Mom is hysterical. Scott is watching the boys while I wait with her, depending on how things go he and I will take turns staying here with Mom."

"Well that's good. That's good," Janice mumbled. Raising her voice she then calmly asked, "How did this happen?"

"The guy who hit him said he was just walking across the freeway. It was a college kid Jan. We're told he's devastated. I feel so sorry for him. I mean who would expect an elderly man to be walking across the freeway? I mean not a street but the middle of the damn freeway!"

"What freeway? Why was Pop walking across the freeway?"

"Mom said he was going to sit by the lake; it's a beautiful day which we don't get many of this time of year. She said he likes to watch the birds. There's a pedestrian overpass for people to cross the freeway. Mom said he always complained that it was too long to walk. I guess he decided to take a shortcut and cross the freeway instead. Crazy. I mean who would cross a damn freeway on foot? Scott and I feel really sorry for the kid who hit him."

"That's awful."

Without hesitation Marge replied, "It's probably his drinking spot Jan. I mean watch the birds? Give me a break. I never thought of Dad as a nature lover." Then Marge took a long pause before continuing, "I don't have the heart to say anything to Mom; she believes his bullshit. Jan, he was probably drunk and didn't know what he was doing. That's the only explanation I can think of."

"If he was drunk the doctors would have told you that. They test people for that stuff Marge. We don't know what happened yet. Let's wait and see."

Marge sighed, knowing she and Janice would never see their father the same way-- or their mother, with whom Marge became fairly close once she was old enough to feel badly for her. They had long ago agreed not to talk about their parents. "I think you should come home. I think you should get on the first flight you can. Ask Richard to come with you."

Flustered, Janice swiftly responded, "I can't. I'm inundated at work. I just can't pick up and leave right now. I have too many responsibilities; too many commitments. What good would it do if I was there? There's nothing I can do. Richard can't do anything, and he couldn't leave work even if he wanted to. Richard doesn't even know Dad. And you don't even know what's what at this point."

After a long pause during which Marge tried to collect her thoughts she said, "Mom could use the support Jan."

"I'll call her. I will. I'll call her as soon as you let me know she's back in the house. If things get worse I'll come but I can't drop everything now; I have no choice. Try to understand."

Annoyed but not surprised Marge replied, "I'll call you later and let you know what's going on. Please think about coming. I could use you here too Jan."

"Ok. Keep me posted. Take care of yourself," Janice whispered.

"Will do. Bye."

"Bye." As Janice hung up the phone she felt a bit dizzy so she stood for a few moments, just balancing, trying to reclaim her equilibrium. Then she walked back into the dining room, sat down in front of her computer, opened her "memoir notes" file and began working.

At 5:30 Kyle came home. "Hey Mom," he shouted as he walked upstairs to his room.

"Hi," she said from the dining room where she sat mesmerized by her computer screen.

Half an hour later Richard came home. He had something big going on at work and had spent most of the day in his office. He walked past her on his way to the kitchen. "Should we order Chinese?" he asked as he twisted the cap off of a small bottle of Vitamin water. "Sure, that's fine. I'll have my usual."

"Is Kyle here?"

"Yes, he's in his room," she said without diverting her eyes from her computer.

"Kyle. Kyyyle," Richard shouted.

"Yeah Dad," he replied from the top of the stairs.

"We're ordering Chinese. What do you want?"

"Beef and broccoli and some of those ravioli, the fried ones. Thanks."

"Ok." And with that Richard picked up the phone, dialed 3 on their speed dial, and placed their order.

An hour later they quietly ate dinner together, all seated at one end of the table as Janice's folders occupied the other. They used paper plates. After dinner Kyle went to his room for the rest of the evening while Richard watched a football game in the living room, and Janice watched a PBS special on Irish step dancing in bed. At 11:30 Richard came up to their room. Without speaking they both carried out their nightly routine of swapping the bathroom sink to brush their teeth. When Richard turned out the lights and got into bed Janice said, "My father was in an accident today. He was hit by a car."

"That's terrible," Richard said loudly, turning to her. Lying on her back facing the ceiling Janice replied, "Yeah, Marge is really upset. It's bad."

"Is he going to be ok?"

"Don't know."

"How did it happen?"

"I don't know. He was just crossing the street," she softly said. With that she turned onto her side, with her back facing Richard and said, "Good night." He lay looking at her back for a moment and then said, "Good night," while turning onto his side, and back-to-back they fell asleep.

The next day Janice was in her office at 8:15 am.

*

Having called in sick for only the second time since starting at WISE (the first time she had eaten some bad tuna sushi for dinner which caused her to wake up at 3:00 am and left her unable to get off the toilet until after noon the next day), Prilly spent the day lying on her couch, curled up under a pink chenille blanket, watching talk shows and court TV. She kept thinking Pete would call to apologize, but he didn't. As the hours rolled on she started to think about the things he said to her. Maybe she was being irrational. He was allowed to have friends. By evening Prilly was sure that she had blown it. She had overreacted. She wanted to call to tell him but felt frozen. She didn't know what to say, and she was embarrassed. By late evening her thoughts drifted from Pete to work. She started to wonder how she would be able to go to the office the next day. She felt like crap. She wasn't ready to face the world. She decided to set her alarm for the usual 6:00 am and take it from there. When the alarm went off in the morning, she felt too depressed to get out of bed. She called in sick again and watched a "People's Court" marathon on TV while napping intermittently on her couch.

Wednesday morning when she arrived at work at 9:15 Janice immediately cornered her in her office, walking right into the open door without knocking or saying a word. "Oh, hi Janice. How are you?"

"Is everything alright Prilly?" Janice asked in a demanding voice as she sat at the chair across from her.

"Yeah, everything's fine…" before she could continue Janice sternly asked, "Well where have you been? I've been swamped here, neck deep in our series and you've been nowhere to be found."

"I was home sick. I had the flu. I called in."

"Well you should have called or emailed me too Prilly. I mean we're working together now and I need to be able to count on you. Authors are emailing me queries, agents are sending me proposals, and you're nowhere to be found. I've been on my own dealing with all of this and with all of my other responsibilities. I've emailed you several times."

Prilly had no idea why Janice seemed so angry; it wasn't as if she had missed any scheduled meetings with her or any deadlines.

"I haven't checked my email yet. Sorry if you've been stuck because I was out. I was really sick and there's no way I could have come in. I never miss work, you know that. Anyway, I'm sorry.

"Uh huh," Janice replied in a sharp tone while nodding. She then stood up and said, "Please deal with the emails I forwarded to you."

"Ok," Prilly said as Janice walked to the door.

Right before Janice left, she turned to face Prilly and said, "I'm just looking out for you Prilly. People were talking, wondering where you were. I don't want to see you under the gun." With that she walked out leaving Prilly to sit there wondering why she had ever agreed to work with Janice and whether or not people really had been talking.

Prilly spent the rest of the week trying to concentrate on work. She stayed in the office until after 8:30 pm Wednesday, Thursday and Friday. Janice thought Prilly was trying to show that she was on top of things. Really, Prilly was wasting so much time during the day because she was unable to focus— time spent daydreaming about Pete and berating herself— that she needed the extra time in order to get a bare minimum of work done. She also couldn't stand to be alone in her apartment, waiting for the phone to ring. Even though just a month earlier spending time alone in her apartment would have been fine, everything was different now, and every minute spent alone there she wished she was with Pete. In those long solitary moments she grew to blame herself even more. She had tasted happiness and spit it out, afraid to swallow.

Saturday morning she slept until 11:00 am. She wasn't going to bother to shower with nowhere to go, but as she drank her coffee wearing the robe that had recently become her at-home uniform, she decided to do something drastic. She would just show up at the teahouse Pete frequented. Maybe she could accidentally bump into him. She knew it was pathetic and hated herself a little for wanting to do it, but after two hours getting ready (making sure her hair was shiny and her outfit was artsy-sexy-casual) she was approaching the teahouse.

Her heart was racing, and her palms were sweaty. She feared passing out. "This might be a mistake. This might be a really big mistake," echoed in her head when her hand reached for the door, now so sweaty that she left a perspiration handprint on the gold knob as she walked in. She hurried to the counter so fast, as to appear casual, that she didn't scan the whole room to see if he was there. When it was her turn in line she stuttered saying, "Uh, uh, I'll have a, a latte, non-fat. Uh, small please."

As she stood waiting for her beverage she noticed Melville sitting in the front right hand corner by the window. He was writing in a spiral notebook and didn't seem to notice her. As she went to the condiment counter to get a napkin she discretely scoured the place to discover that Pete wasn't there. She felt stupid. She decided to go over to Melville, though she didn't know what he did or didn't know about her and Pete, which made her even more anxious.

"Hi," she said standing right next to Melville.

He shuddered, so engrossed in his notebook that he hadn't noticed her. "Oh, oh hi. Hi Prilly," he stammered, as he closed his notebook and slipped it into an old backpack beside him.

Suddenly with no idea what to say or do Prilly said, "Oh well I noticed you were here so I just wanted to say hi. I have some work to do; so I'm going to go sit down over there," while accidentally pointing to the overcrowded back of the teahouse; there wasn't a free seat in sight. Melville didn't notice. As she started to turn around he said, "You can sit here if you want."

"Oh, sure, thanks," she said as she pulled out the chair next to her which made several squeaking noises. She placed her latte on the table to learn the table was wobbling. Nervous to begin with her, now slippery hands knocked the mug a bit, and some of her drink spilled on the table.

"Oh, that's ok," Melville said as he placed his napkin over the spill.

"Thanks," she said sitting down. "So," she continued staring straight into Melville's eyes; in turn causing him to look down at his hands, "What are you up to?"

"I'm waiting for Pete. Aren't you?" he replied.

Realizing that Melville didn't know they had broken up Prilly started to feel her heart race with excitement. She would see Pete. At any minute he would be walking in. And if Melville didn't know about their fight, maybe it wasn't as bad as she had thought. Maybe it would be ok. Noticing that the silence between his words and her response was too long she quickly said, "No, no I don't have plans to meet him. I was just in the neighborhood. I'm going to an art show later; so I thought I'd grab a coffee and do a little work while I have time to kill."(She instantly regretted the art show lie as it would be hard to keep up if he asked for details).

Before Melville could respond Prilly heard Pete's unmistakable voice shout, "Hey." As she turned her head she realized he wasn't alone. Next to him stood a tall woman with long red hair, dressed all in black with a dog collar necklace tightly wrapped around her pale neck. She looked like she was twenty. "Oh, hey you," Pete said, now noticing Prilly.

"Hi," Prilly said, not knowing what to do. "Hey, I'm glad to see you," he replied. "Melville, Prilly, this is my friend Veronica."

"Hi, nice to meet you," Prilly said as she extended her hand out in horror.

"Hey, yeah, you too," Veronica said, keeping her hands in her pockets. "Pete, I gotta go, I'm gonna be late. I'll call you later," she continued.

"Ok, Hon," Pete said as he hugged her goodbye. "I'm gonna get an espresso. You two all set?"

Prilly and Melville nodded awkwardly and Pete was off. The next four minutes felt like an eternity as Prilly tried to acclimate herself to what was happening. She had a splitting pain in her stomach and was afraid she would be sick. She imagined herself unable to leave the toilet in the one-person bathroom with mobs of tea drinkers pounding on the door.

When Pete walked back to the table he stood between Prilly and Melville because there weren't any free chairs around.

Terrified of what he might say Prilly blurted out, "I was just stopping in for a coffee on my way to plans I have and I saw Melville so…"

With his characteristic close-mouthed smile that this time made him look sexier than she had remembered he said, "Well I'm glad to see you. I've been meaning to call you but, but you know."

"Yeah, yeah I know. Well I have to go," she said jumping up.

"Don't leave. Why don't you join us? We're going to a poetry reading."

"Oh, thanks, but I really can't. I have plans. Some other time," she replied as she frantically tried to grab her bag off the floor without knocking the table and spilling more coffee. "Thanks anyway. Good seeing you. Bye. Bye Melville," she hurriedly stammered as she walked towards the door.

"Prill, you sure?" Pete shouted after her.

"Yeah, yeah, I have plans, sorry. Good to see you."

"Ok, bye," he said, now smiling ear to ear.

Prilly hopped in a cab outside the teahouse and went back to her apartment. She spent the rest of the day thinking about how pathetic she was, how sexy Pete was, whether or not she should have gone with them, and whether or not he was sleeping with Veronica. When all of the other thoughts started to quiet down, the last one overtook her. She fell asleep on her couch watching a Hallmark movie about a woman who battled a health insurance company to get an experimental breast cancer treatment. The woman died.

At 7:00 am she was awoken by her telephone ringing. She fumbled into the kitchen and picked up the receiver.

"Hello," she answered sleepily.

"Hey you. Did I wake you?" Pete asked.

"Yeah, it's ok though," she whispered as she wondered if he tried to make his voice so impossibly sexy or if it just was naturally.

"Sorry. I thought your machine would get it if you were sleeping. I've been up all night. I couldn't stop thinking about you. Come over, ok?"

Prilly stood frozen. Like a child climbing a tree, 'just one branch higher' while too scared to look down, she knew it was dangerous but she kept clinging, afraid to let go. After a moment passed she said, "I have to shower and stuff, I'll come over later."

"Ok. Hurry."

*

Three hours later Prilly arrived at Pete's apartment. He greeted her in his boxer shorts, bathrobe and signature smile. "Hey. Come on in. I have something for you. I wrote you a short story," he said as she followed him into the bedroom. "It's right there," he said pointing to the bed. "I'll get you some coffee while you read it. I worked on it all week."

Prilly made her way to the bed, dropped her oversized handbag on the floor (in which she had put a makeup bag, toothbrush, and change of underwear just in case) and picked up the papers. There were two single-spaced pages.

By the time Pete had come over to her with a mug of coffee she had finished reading. It was a beautifully written piece about a man who wandered into a graveyard at night to protect the "sleeping dead." She didn't understand at all how this could be for her; she tried to think of it as a metaphor or allegory but any connection to her or to them completely eluded her.

"What do you think?" he asked, sitting down on the edge of the bed.

"It's beautiful. Your writing is like a painting; I can see it all so clearly."

He blushed, looking down. "I paint with words."

"Thank you for giving it to me." Sitting there next to him she felt just as alive as she had when they first met, but now her head was spinning with questions, fears and doubt. She still didn't know what had happened, why he hadn't called all week, and who Veronica was. "I've been really upset since, since what happened last weekend."

"Let's just forget about it. People overreact. I'm sorry I shouted at you. I was hurt. I thought you knew how I felt about you so I felt insulted."

Wishing he would elaborate she said, "I'm sorry if I overreacted too."

He leaned to her, rubbed the tip of his nose to hers, and then leaned back and smiled. Prilly looked down and asked, "Who was that woman yesterday?" and then looked up, waiting for an answer.

Pete smiled again and said, "Just a friend. She's just a friend."

PART TWO

CHAPTER 6

Kyle Goldwyn was not an average seventeen year old. Despite his mother's secret anxiety that he may be below average in almost every conceivable way, Kyle was, secretly, quite exceptional. He was enormously perceptive. Even more so, he not only saw things that other people seemed to miss, but he saw them in remarkable ways.

At the age of three a much larger four and half a year old boy at his preschool bullied him. When Kyle built a block fortress the other boy came and kicked it down while mocking him. One day the other boy pushed him off of a swing causing him to badly scrape his knees. After Janice repeatedly yelled at the director of the preschool that she would sue her if Kyle was hurt again (yelling to the point where the woman forever cringed at the sight of her), Janice told Kyle to, "Ignore the boy; he's a loser," to which Kyle replied, "I think he must be very unhappy." Janice rolled her eyes fearing Kyle was a wimp. When he was eight years old a discussion about Christmas in his third grade class prompted him to ask his mother why Jesus Christ was killed. Only partly hearing the question she answered, "That's what the bible teaches… that's all, you don't have to agree if you don't," to which Kyle responded, "I think Jesus Christ must have been very special. Maybe his ideas were so special that they frightened people." Janice was so busy opening junk mail at the time that she just said, "Uh huh." Kyle ran upstairs to his room, where, lying on his bed he spent the rest of the afternoon wondering what made good people afraid. During the next several years as Janice schlepped him from museum to museum hoping to 'make him interesting' Kyle started to see the world through different lenses. While Janice got the free audio headset tour for both of them, so that Kyle could "properly" learn about the "great art", he always muted his. He looked at the paintings, sculptures and photographs and tried to imagine where the artist was from, how they grew up, how they came to see the world, and how much of that vision lay before him, lopped off in a frame. This process made him wonder about different cultures and how they produce different kinds of people. He wondered where innovation came from and why some people's work seemed derivative and others seemed to stand on its own, unable to be defined or judged. He came to see beauty in her many guises which so too made him clearly see her falsehoods.

Kyle was also keenly aware of people's emotional centers, as if he could almost feel them immediately. As a kind soul he used this skill only to their advantage, never his own. This gift of perception helped him in innumerable ways, not the least of which was related to his mother. Of all the things that Kyle could perceive in his environment, what he saw most clearly was when there was a need for silence. Therefore Kyle Goldwyn knew that the greatest kindness he could show his mother was not to show her all the things he saw, and so he didn't.

Although quiet and not terribly good looking in the traditional sense, Kyle was not considered unattractive by his peers. Contrary to his parents' assumption, he had dated several girls (including fooling around with several and sleeping with two). He had many friends at school and more importantly no enemies. Outside of school he mostly spent time with his best friend, Sam.

Kyle and Sam hung out in Central Park playing cards; they went to music stores and browsed old vinyl; they walked around the Village talking about the evils of organized religion or politics (they were both fiercely on the left though unimpressed by most politicians and surprisingly missing the idealism often characterized by Leftie youth); they went to parties at friends' houses or met girls at the movies; and most often they went to Sam's place and watched movies (Sam lived in a tiny two bedroom apartment with his mother Melanie, a paralegal at a big Wall Street law firm. She had long blonde hair and Kyle thought she was incredibly beautiful and too young-looking to be a mother, though he knew not to mention this to Sam).

Sometimes they stopped by the NYU dorms to see Kyle's cousin, Natashya. Neither Kyle nor Natashya ever told their parents, but they had become close friends during those brutal family vacation weeks. They texted every week (sometimes daily) and hung out at least once a month since Natashya (Tash as Kyle and Kyle alone called her) moved to New York. When one of them had a problem they wanted to talk about they met at their favorite boisterous deli, where they always waited until a booth opened up, and they shared a platter of blueberry cheese blintzes and a pot of weak coffee they both complained about. Although she looked naïve with a freckled face and preppy clothes that stood out in the artsy punk crowds in her neighborhood, Natashya was a rebel. She used to tell Kyle that she was "sexually free" when he would question why she always seemed to be "hooking up with some random guy." In response she teased him that he was just uptight because they were cousins. He thought that she was a little too free. He feared that she didn't know how foolish she sometimes looked. Natashya also had a fake ID which she used to buy beer for Kyle and Sam. Kyle and Sam never drank more than one or two cans. From time to time she also smoked a joint. Sam always took a hit or two but Kyle never did. This wasn't because he was a "straight edge" as Natashya would say while giggling at him, but rather because he knew that if there were ever an emergency one of them needed to be sober. He only trusted himself with that responsibility.

Kyle was acutely aware of Tash's propensity to morph free-spiritedness into a lack of consideration for others. He didn't let it bother him until Halloween. Natashya invited Kyle and Sam to a party at an underground club. She insisted that they dress in costume. When they arrived at her dorm, both made up to look like mimes, Kyle immediately noticed that Tash seemed a little out of it. Her eyes didn't focus when she offered them a beer while she finished styling her hair. He figured she had smoked a bit. She was wearing a Playboy bunny costume, complete with a white fluffy tail, white fishnet stockings and stripper-style white patent leather stilettos. With her innocent face covered in makeup and her very fine light brown hair long and stick straight, Sam thought she looked hot. She had a Lindsey Lohan look. Kyle thought that a long dress revealing only one bare shoulder was far sexier than a hooker-esque ensemble but he kept this thought to himself to avoid being teased— and called uptight, which he wasn't. Tash was too special to distract the eye in such cliché ways.

"What do you think?" she asked throwing her arms up in one of her over-the-top model poses.

"You look awesome," Sam said enthusiastically.

"Weeell?" she asked looking at Kyle.

"I think you're more beautiful than you know," he answered. She smiled brightly and said, "Let's roll; cabs might be tough tonight."

Three hours later Kyle and Sam were getting bored; the large red club decked out in an excess of black streamers and hanging paper skeletons was massively crowded, and over time the heavy synthesizer sounds of the techno music grated on their nerves.

"Come on, let's get out of here man," Sam said.

"Yeah, ok. I have to find Tash to tell her we're going and make sure she's ok getting a cab on her own."

"I'll wait here."

"Ok," Kyle shouted as he started to make his way through the crowd on the dance floor, as that was the last place he had seen her, which was now over an hour ago. He wandered around, squinting at times when the strobe lights flashed in his face. He stood outside of the women's bathroom for fifteen minutes thinking if she was in there she'd have to pass him when she left. He sent her three text messages without reply. Tash was nowhere to be found. Eventually he made his way back to Sam.

"Hey dude, what happened to you? I didn't think you were coming back."

"Can't find Tash. I don't like just leaving her here. She's probably wasted."

"She brought us here man. I'm sure she can handle herself. Let's go to my place. My mom's out with that jackass again; we can do whatever we want." Kyle often crashed on the small gray futon in Sam's room.

Kyle scanned the room one more time before acquiescing, "Yeah, ok, let's get out of here."

From the subway Kyle sent Tash two more text messages. Never drifting off for more than an hour at a time he checked his phone religiously all night in hopes of a reply.

The next day at 5:00 pm Natashya finally texted: "Hey. Sorry to worry. Met a friend. Hope you had fun. Hugs, T."

Kyle wasn't the type to get angry and certainly not to hold a grudge; however, something in him shifted ever so slightly that night. He never mentioned it to her or to anyone.

*

Halloween proved to be a turning point for Pete and Prilly too. The two had been inseparable since the day Prilly returned to Pete's apartment. She stayed in his apartment from Friday night to Monday morning every week, as well as most weeknights. They made romantics dinners, read poetry and went to movies. They listened to music, drank cheap wine and made love without ever saying the word love. There were only two problems, both of which Pete seemed oblivious to.

First, Prilly's commitment to her work was dwindling as a result of her preoccupation with Pete (combined with utter exhaustion, also caused by her preoccupation with Pete). She had yet to adjust to her routine of racing to and from Pete's and was often late to work. In an effort to spend as much time with him as possible, she tried to rush out of work at the end of the day as well, and she no longer checked her email over the weekend. In short, she was working far fewer hours. Moreover, tired and distracted, when she was at work she wasn't as productive as she had been in the past. She knew that she wasn't getting as much done as she used to but felt it was a small price to pay for finally living a "full life." At the heart of it, though she would never say it out loud, she feared she would never meet anyone else who would make her feel the way she felt with Pete.

Second, she existed just on the edge of worry all the time. She didn't trust Pete. She spent many nights lying awake in bed replaying everything he had said (and not said) that particular day. Every comment became suspect. She was consumed by questions like: "What is the message he is sending me? Is our relationship fizzling? Is he happy? Is there someone else?" That last question never quieted down and would slip into her mind at the most inconvenient times, like when she was in a meeting with Janice, when she was talking on the phone with her family and when she was looking in the mirror searching for flaws to cover up. The louder the voice in her head, the more flaws she found. Pete didn't help matters by continuing to flirt with every young attractive woman he saw-- right in front of Prilly. Nights dancing at clubs that had once felt magical now were a game of "I spy" gone awry for Prilly. "I spy a slut. I spy Pete looking at the slut. I spy Pete talking to the slut." All of the spying was exhausting. If trying to be interesting was tiring, trying to be *more* interesting than every other woman in their path was utterly depleting. Fearing that many of them were prettier than she was, she felt she had no choice. Sometimes she thought that Pete knew how worried she was; at times she actually thought he tried to make her jealous. During happy moments he said things like, "I'm happy with you…well right now at least," followed by his signature close-mouthed smile, and laugh. He made comments like, "That woman is beautiful don't you think? Her bone structure is phenomenal," leaving Prilly to just stare at him in astonishment, not sure of how to play it. She once asked him if he was trying to make her feel insecure, and he laughed at her and said, "Only you can make yourself feel insecure. That's not on me girl." She never brought it up again; not until Halloween.

Halloween fell on a Friday night. Pete wanted to go to a costume party a friend of his was hosting. When trying to convince Prilly to go with him Pete proclaimed his friend Luke, "Is a wonderful cartoonist, very cutting-edge; he does wonderful things with strong female characters that you'd love. He's a bit of an opiate boy, but hey, everyone's got a monkey on their back right?"

"What? Opiates as in opium? As in heroine? Uh, no," Prilly said, horrified at both the information and the casual way that Pete always revealed tidbits like this. "Not everyone has a drug addiction or anything like it. I don't know about going to this guy's place. It doesn't sound good."

Pete rolled his eyes and in his most annoyed voice said, "He's not an addict, he uses occasionally. He's got it managed. Not everyone who dabbles is an addict; don't believe everything they tell you on the ten o'clock news. He's an artist and he's very successful. He's fabulous. I shouldn't have mentioned anything, and you would have gone and had a wonderful time. Step outside the box girl."

Prilly wondered if she was being provincial. She loved art, and now she had a chance to hang out with a cool artist crowd; why was she looking for problems? At moments like this she also questioned what Pete saw in her at all; he seemed to think she was limited, and sometimes he made her feel that way. She never quite knew if it was she who couldn't get outside of traditional thinking or if in fact he just had a very convenient way of justifying bad behavior, including his own. Every time she started to really think it was him, he said something cutting that got her right at her insecurity-center, and she refocused on herself. Even though she started to notice the pattern, she still didn't know if it was her or him. Ultimately she wanted to believe it was her problem so that she could fix it.

Per Pete's suggestion they dressed up as Sid and Nancy. This simply required Pete to spike his hair a bit and pretty much wear the same black vinyl pants and white T-shirt he normally wore on weekends, kicked up a notch with an old black leather jacket. Prilly wore a blonde wig Pete had in one of his drawers. She didn't ask why he had it, not wanting to know. She wore tight black jeans and a long sleeved black shirt with a sequined black leather choker around her neck and an armful of silver bangles she bought in the children's section of a drugstore. She did her makeup severely with dark black liquid eyeliner and hot pink lipstick. "Wow girl, you look very punk meets pop art!"

"What does that mean? I don't look stupid do I?"

"You look terrific."

In the cab on the way to the party Prilly thought to herself that playing dress up was actually fun. She decided to forget the nonsense about the guy whose party it was and just have a good time. She leaned against Pete and held his hand bumping her head on his chin as they plowed over potholes.

They walked into the party hand-in-hand which made Prilly feel like the luckiest woman there. The industrial style loft with exposed brick and silver pipes hanging from the ceiling was surprisingly big. "Pete was right this guy is successful," Prilly thought. There were large windows but unfortunately they overlooked the building next door. Dimmed red light bulbs in lamps around the apartment complemented the seductive background music. As they made their way through the crowd of thirty or forty people a guy wearing a long sleeve electric blue shirt, unbuttoned a third of the way down his hairy chest, and skintight black jeans grabbed Pete's arm shouting, "Hey man, hey, you came, phenomenal."

"Hey Luke. Your new place is wooonderful. Those pieces, are they yours?" Pete asked pointing to the left.

"Yeah, yeah, I did those ages ago. I'm too lazy to frame anything new."

Feeling self-conscious just standing there Prilly casually rubbed her hand against Pete's arm. "Oh, Luke this is my girlfriend Prilly."

Prilly smiled and put her hand out, "It's nice to meet you. Your apartment is great."

Luke grabbed Prilly by the shoulders and kissed her on both cheeks. Before Prilly could say anything else Pete said with a laugh, "So what's your costume man?"

"Fuck that," Luke replied. "I'm me man. I'm just me," and with that he walked off; Prilly watched him grab someone else exuberantly. "See, he's all right," Pete said.

"Sure. This place is really cool," she said looking around the room.

"Let me find the bar, what'll you have? Some wine?"

"Sure, that'd be great. But I'll come with you," she said, not wanting to be alone in a crowd of people that she didn't know.

"Hey. See that spot on the leather couch," he said pointing to the other end of the room, "go grab us a seat, and I'll be right back."

"Ok," she said as they parted ways.

Twenty minutes later, after two awkward exchanges, one with a guy who wanted to debate whether or not Mighty Mouse had been on cocaine and the other with a gay couple who asked her if she could move over (leaving her squished in the corner of the couch), she started to have a mental meltdown wondering where Pete was. Just as she decided to get up to go look for him, she noticed him walking towards her. He was with a beautiful woman dressed in a long white flowing see-through dress with green petals on it (that she would soon realize matched her exquisite eyes), white face makeup and very long brown hair with long side-swept bangs across her forehead nearly covering one eye. As they approached, with Pete smiling, she already knew what he was going to say.

"Prilly, this is my friend Clyde."

Prilly could feel every part of her insides twitching. She was hot and a bit dizzy. Clyde was even more beautiful than she had imagined. "And for Christ's sake," she thought, "she's dressed as Ophelia. Ophelia!" she silently screamed. It couldn't get worse.

"Here," Pete said as he handed Prilly a small plastic cup of red wine, also keeping one for himself. She outstretched her hand and as she took the cup said, "Hi, it's nice to meet you."

"You too," Clyde said in a voice Prilly feared was as lovely as her face.

"Clyde's dressed up like Ophelia. It's wonderful don't you think?" Pete asked smiling.

"Yeah, yeah. I thought it was Ophelia. It's great," she stammered, desperately trying to conceal how shaken she was.

"Clyde's here with a friend, he's in the kitchen trying to make a martini without vermouth," Pete said as he started to laugh. Clyde looked at him and smiled.

"Wouldn't that just be vodka?" Prilly asked before nervously taking a gulp of her wine.

Pete and Clyde burst into laughter. Prilly didn't know what was so funny but she felt stupid, left out and increasingly nauseous.

"Well, it was nice to meet you," Clyde said as her laughter subsided. Then she turned to Pete and said, "I'll talk to you later," before giving him a peck on the cheek.

"Sure," he said.

"Nice meeting you too," Prilly said as Clyde walked away.

"Hey, move over girl," Pete said, indicating he wanted to sit down.

"There's no room. I had saved you a seat but it's too crowded; I couldn't hold it."

"No worries," he said as he sat down on the wide arm of the couch just to her left. "Sorry I got held up. I bumped into Clyde in the kitchen when I was getting our drinks. She started telling me about some wonderful new band she's discovered, blah, blah, blah. I didn't want to be rude."

"It's ok," Prilly softly replied.

Pete leaned in and with his free hand touched her chin and kissed her.

They stayed at the party for nearly four hours during which time they chatted with Luke, talked to cartoonists and musicians, flipped through photography books, nibbled on hummus, pita chips and olives and occasionally held hands. Through all this, although they didn't see her again, Prilly had a singular thought: Clyde.

*

In the cab ride back to Pete's, which Prilly thought of as "home", she agonized over whether or not to say something to him. She couldn't get Clyde out of her mind and she was terrified of blurting something out that she wouldn't be able to take back. Biting her tongue she sat quietly all the way back, holding Pete's hand as he leaned his head on hers.

When they got back to his place Pete put some soft music on. Smiling he said, "Come here." She went over to his extended arms; he took her hands in his and started to sway back and forth. She leaned into his chest and they danced. Overcome by a wave of emotion, "Did you know she'd be there?" slipped out in a hushed voice.

"What?" he asked, leaning back while still holding onto her hands.

"Clyde. Did you know she was going to be there? Because if you..."

He cut her off with, "This is what you're thinking about?" as he let go of her hands. "This is what you're thinking about while we're having this wonderful night?" he asked in a disgusted tone as he walked into the kitchen.

Mad at herself for ruining the moment, and mad at him, she stood there and said in a louder voice, "Well if you knew she was going to be there I just think you should have warned me."

"Oh fuck Prilly," he said as he opened the refrigerator and started looking at the nearly empty shelves, "What's the difference? No, I didn't know she was gonna be there. I mean I guess I knew it was pooossible; she knows Luke; she knows lots of people I know, but she didn't like teeell me she was going to be there or anything," he finished as he shut the refrigerator door.

"Well, I just felt caught off guard. I think you should have told me she might be there."

Now filling a glass with tap water he said, "I was there with you. She was there with some guy. What's the difference? I wanted to avoid this. I didn't see any reason to get you all freaked out when for all I knew she wouldn't even be there. I know how insecure you are about this," he said in a hostile tone as he shut off the tap and started drinking.

"Fuck you. I would never bring you to a party where my ex was without warning you. You disappear for ages and then bang, I'm faced with you and your ex."

"Fuck me? Fuck me?" he yelled now staring straight at her through the cut out wall. "Fuck you!"

With that Prilly frantically grabbed her overnight bag from the floor and stormed into the bathroom where she shoved her makeup and toothbrush into the bag and then left the apartment in a frenzy, slamming the door behind her.

*

Prilly was falling over herself and her bag down the stairs as she tried to quickly get out of Pete's building. Her insides were racing and she felt like she was on fire. As she flung the building door open and felt a wave of cold air smack her face she heard, "Wait... Prill, wait."

She turned around to see Pete standing there. "Don't go like this. Let's not end things like this."

She stood motionless trying to resist both the urge to tell him to go to hell and the urge to run into his arms. She wanted to leave as a sign of pride, but she was afraid that if she did it might be for good. So she just stood.

"Hey, come on. It's cold out there. Come back inside. I'm sorry I shouted. Come inside."

Prilly stepped back into the building and followed Pete to his apartment. But there was no going back.

Over the next six weeks Prilly started to unravel. She was consumed by jealous impulses. When Pete was in the shower she glanced at his Blackberry. When glances didn't suffice, she scrolled through his emails, texts and phone logs. Sometimes when his apartment phone rang she answered it; knowing that would probably bother him, she never mentioned those calls. To compensate for her fears, she tried to spend as much time as possible with Pete. She tried to be interesting, she tried to be sexy and mostly she just tried to be there. No longer wanting to run home after work to get an overnight bag and freshen up, she now brought a makeup case to work and left two drawers full of clothes at Pete's. She rushed out of the office as quickly as possible and raced to meet him. Every time she caught him chatting up another woman she found a way to punish him without telling him why.

One Friday night when she arrived at the teahouse he was sitting and reading something he had written to some woman. Prilly went out of her way to be rude to the woman, who, taking the hint, left abruptly. Pete smirked and said, "Hey girl, she noticed my drawing and asked what it was, and so we ended up having a nice little chat, and I read her something, that's all," to which Prilly responded, "I don't care." She put on a happy face that night and then went out of her way to be disagreeable for the rest of the weekend. She refused to go to a house party he wanted to pop in on; she told him the art at a gallery they went to was ugly after he said he loved it; and, she made enough noise in the mornings to disrupt his sleep without appearing like she was trying to wake him. Worse than anything she was doing to Pete was the mental anguish she was putting herself through. Every time the phone in his apartment rang she imagined it was Clyde, but on this, and this alone, she bit her tongue. And then one Friday afternoon she got a call at work.

"Hello."

"Hey Babe."

"Pete?"

"Yeah, of course."

"Oh, it's just that you've never called me at work before. Is everything ok?"

"Yeah, everything is fine. Listen, I need to ask you to spend the night at your place. I have a situation I need to deal with."

"What's wrong?" Prilly asked solemnly.

"Nothing girl, just got to take care of something. Come over tomorrow night and we'll spend the rest of the weekend together, all right?"

"Ok, sure. I hope nothing is wrong. If you need something call me."

"Thanks. Bye."

"Bye." With that Prilly hung up the phone wondering what was going on. She was filled with questions that all asked the same things: "Is this about me? Is this about us?"

That night Prilly returned to her apartment for the first night in weeks. The first thing she noticed was a foul stench coming from her kitchen. She hadn't taken the garbage out in weeks, and something in there reeked. As she pulled the drawstring bag out of the plastic barrel she nearly hurled. She looked at the bottles under her kitchen sink desperate for an odor-eating product of some kind. Absent anything like that she grabbed a bottle of perfume and sprayed some in each room of her small apartment. It didn't help. She sat on her couch deciding whether or not to order Chinese food and thinking about Pete. "What is going on with him? Why didn't he say why he cancelled?" As she sat she became increasingly agitated. The putrid smell in her apartment was taunting her. She shouldn't be there. She should be at Pete's. She thought about going down to the teahouse in his neighborhood to accidentally run into him, if he was there. Knowing it was too transparent she decided to order some food and curl up on the couch. An hour later she was sitting and eating chicken in a spicy brown sauce with chopsticks, right out of the container while watching a Lifetime movie about a woman who had an affair with her best friend's husband. She drank half a bottle of red wine and passed out in her work clothes.

The next morning she went through the motions of her former morning routine— French roast coffee and her favorite New York website. She wasn't really looking for something to do; she was just passing time until her plans with Pete, whenever that would be. By this time she wasn't particularly eager to spend time with him but she was desperate to find out how he had spent the evening. After a night of panic she had tried to convince herself that it must be something benign and she was freaking out for nothing. If he was spending the night with another woman he would have made up some excuse, but he hadn't. It must be nothing.

After showering and getting ready she sat on her couch trying to figure out what to do. She was having a really good hair day, and her outfit was spot-on. She was wearing a long sleeve black sheath-style dress with black tights and new mauve maryjane style high heels. She felt like she looked really good and didn't want to sit at home wasting it. She wanted Pete to see her before the end of the day when undoubtedly she'd be more haggard-looking.

She decided to throw some work in a bag and go to the teahouse near Pete's. Janice had been on her case to mark-up the drafts of the first three memoirs that came in, and with any luck she'd bump into Pete while she still looked good.

An hour later and a block away from the teahouse her hands began to tingle. This feeling had become familiar so she knew it would soon pass. As she approached the teahouse she saw Pete coming out. Just as her adrenaline was pumping hard with wonder about his reaction to seeing her, Clyde emerged from the door. Tremors coursed through her body as Pete turned and saw her. She wanted to turn and run away but concerned with saving face she kept moving forward.

"Prilly, hey, what are you doing in this neck of the woods? You remember my friend Clyde," he said as he touched Clyde's arm.

"I had some work to do and, and there's a problem in my apartment so, so I just thought I'd come and get some work done.

My apartment reeks. It's unbearable and I need to work. I didn't think I'd see you."

"I was just going to walk Clyde to the subway but if you wait I'll come back after," Pete said as if nothing was wrong.

"Pete was nice enough to help me out with something last night. I thought the least I could do was take him for a coffee," Clyde interjected, gently brushing her long bangs from her eye.

Unable to stop thinking about how beautiful Clyde was Prilly's tremors morphed into full-on waves of rage. Clearly sensing Prilly was upset Pete said, "Yeah, I'll tell you about it in a bit, ok? Wait for me."

Unable to control herself she blurted out, "No, no I don't think so. I'm not going to wait," and she turned around and started to walk away so quickly that she twice tripped on her own feet. Pete hollered after her, "Hang on there," but Prilly just threw one of her arms up in disgust and kept walking.

When she got home she went straight into her bedroom where she lay on the bed too worked up to fall asleep. A few hours later Pete called. As soon as he said "hello" she screamed "fuck you" on top of her lungs and hung up. She waited for him to call back but he didn't. Prilly knew it was over.

Janice was receiving updates from Marge, at whose insistence she also began making Sunday phone calls to her mother during the weeks after her father was hospitalized. The Sunday following Halloween was particularly stressful for Janice. Her father had finally been released a few days earlier. He was wheelchair bound and forced to use a catheter to go to the bathroom, which, like many other things, Myra had been trained to assist with. When she hung up the phone with Marge, who again urged her to visit (to which Janice replied, "I'm just swamped at work; it's a bad time") she leaned against her kitchen wall and paused before making the dreaded weekly call to her mother. After hearing things like, "Dad's in diapers Jan, diapers," from her sister, she knew it would be a brutal call.

"Hello," Myra answered.

"Hi Mom."

"Oh, hi Jan."

"How's Dad?"

"Oh, not so good."

"Why? What's wrong Ma?"

"It's much harder for him now being at home. I thought he would be happy to have his foods again and watch his TV. You know he couldn't watch his programs at the hospital. The other man in his room-- he didn't have his own room you know; we couldn't do anything about it-- the other man in his room would sleep all the time and your father couldn't watch his programs. Scott brought him some headset contraption to use to watch his programs but he wouldn't have any of it. So..."

"Mom, Mom," Janice interrupted, frustrated that she had to hear yet again that her father was forced to share a room in the hospital, which she was convinced was just a tactic her mother used for pointing out the fact that she hadn't visited, "Mom, you were telling me how Pop is."

"Oh, right. Well I thought he'd be happy to have his programs and his food, I made him the noodle casserole he likes so much but he hardly ate any of it. He usually takes two or three portions; this time he only had a few bites. I even put those fried onions on top that he likes so much. I made him creamed potatoes which you know he can't resist and Jell-O, the red Jell-O, and nothing. Just a few bites. I made him eat some chicken soup Ellie from next door brought over but... he just sits in his chair in the living room or sleeps."

"Uh huh."

"I don't think he likes me taking care of him, you know. It was easier in the hospital. There's a nurse coming to the house once a day to check on him but that's only for another week or so. Her name is Betsey. He can't be alone you know. So I can't leave the house unless Betsey is here, or your sister and Scott. And he's so stubborn, you know your father."

"Do you need money Mom? I might be able to get a little something together to send you? You could hire someone to help you."

"No, no Jan. We're ok. We're just fine."

"You can't do it forever Mom. Not like this. People don't need to live like this nowadays. You can hire help."

"I know, I know. We'll see. We'll see what happens. Each day as it comes, like I always say."

"Uh huh. Right Mom. It sounds like Pop is just a little depressed. It's a big change. Or maybe he's in pain. Is he in a lot of pain? Does he have the right medication?"

"He doesn't say much you know. He's on all these pills, and I have to keep track of them. I think he's just tired mostly."

"I'm sure he'll be better soon Ma. I have to go; I have work I have to do but I'll call you next Sunday. You can call me if you need something."

"You have to work; it's Sunday. You work too hard. You need to take care of yourself Jannie. I worry about you. And..."

Janice cut her off saying, "I know, I know Mom. I'm fine, I'm just busy. I really have to go. I'll call you next Sunday. Tell Pop I said hi."

"Ok, bye. I love you."

"Bye." And with that Janice hung up. She took a deep breath and walked over to a bowl of fruit on her kitchen counter. She shuffled the fruit around and grabbed an apple which she polished on her shirt as she walked over to the dining room table. She stood staring at her computer for a moment and then made a beeline across the hall and into the living room. She manually turned on the television, sat down in the middle of the couch and watched the last half of a jazz retrospective.

After six weeks Janice decided this torturous weekly call to her mother was the most unpleasant development in her life in recent memory. Janice didn't adjust to change well generally; nor did she deal well with family issues. Growing up in a house in which things could quickly shift at any moment, she had learned the value of routine and distance. While it was easy to put geographic space in between her and "them", she became well skilled at creating other distances too. Her discomfort with any disruption to her normal schedule could not be seen outwardly by anyone because, true to type, Janice never discussed any problems she may be facing. However, although they might not know the cause, everyone who encountered Janice could see the manifestations of her angst. Richard sensed he should work even later than usual. He also knew it wasn't the best time to make dinner arrangements with colleagues. He knew this just by observing the energy with which Janice would shut kitchen cabinet doors. Unfortunately though, unable to see her heart, he couldn't see when it was broken. Kyle knew it was time for invisibility. He, and he alone, knew his mother was sad, not angry, even though he didn't know why. So he spent as much time outside of the house as was possible, doing his duty of being neither seen nor heard. Her colleagues knew she was "in a way" because she sighed loudly as she walked from her office to the copy machine; she threw the leftover part of her tuna sandwich in the receptionist area garbage without bothering to seal the Ziploc bag it was in, thus stinking up the office; and worst of all she popped her head into people's offices to say things like, "Watch out, I hear the guys are making cuts, trimming the fat." When it came to these kinds of jabs, Prilly was on Janice's radar more than anyone else.

Kyle hadn't seen Tash since Halloween. They sent each other text messages sporadically. Tash was busy with finals and didn't have time to hang out and Kyle was happy to have a break, though at times he thought of her and wondered what she was up to. The Saturday before Christmas Kyle received a text: "Hey stranger. Gotta go home for the big Xmas family-thing. Free tomorrow am? Wanna meet at the usual for blintzes? Much to catch up on." Kyle responded, "Yeah, c u at 11."

The next morning on his way to meet Tash, Kyle stopped at the base of the staircase when he thought he heard his mother on the telephone. She sounded strange. He stood quietly and listened to what he gathered was the tail end of a conversation. His mother was speaking in a hushed tone reserved for the most private or troubling exchanges.

"I can't do that. I can't do that Marge."

"I'm sorry. I told you weeks ago that we've been invited to a Christmas dinner with Richard's colleagues. He said we have to go. It's important; it's business."

"Uh, huh."

"I know, I know. I just can't do it. I'll explain to Mom again when I talk to her tomorrow. And I've sent her some money."

"Yeah, ok. Bye."

When Janice hung up the phone she stood, perfectly still. Kyle waited for the sound of movement, for a sound that indicated she was all right but he heard nothing. He thought about going over to her and asking if she was ok. His father had told him that his grandfather had been in an accident. The day he told him Kyle went to his mother and said, "I heard about your dad; I'm really sorry." She said, "Oh, thank you. I'm fine." No one ever said a word to him about it after that and he didn't ask. His mother had always been very weird about her family. They never saw his grandparents; although his grandmother faithfully sent him birthday, Christmas and Easter cards, each with fifteen dollars in them. The fifteen dollars, his mother's silence and quips Marge had made over the years all told him that his grandparents probably weren't well off. He knew there was more to it but he didn't probe. He liked Marge a lot the few times she had visited. She was fun and down-to-earth, and she told him funny stories about his mom which he'd otherwise never know. She also swore quite a bit, which he found refreshing. He wished she visited more. He wished to know his mothers' family.

After standing and waiting for a noise indicating that his mom was ok he decided to leave. Instead of just taking off as he usually did, he shouted, "Bye Mom, going out with Tash, see you later."

Startled, Janice leapt from the kitchen wall that she was propped against and hollered back "bye" as he was locking the door behind him. She hadn't heard who he was going out with.

Twenty minutes later Kyle walked into the deli surprised to see Tash was already sitting in a booth. She started smiling and waving as soon as she saw him, reminding him how much fun they had together. As he approached the table she jumped up and hugged him.

"Dude, it's been so long. Crazy."

"No, no way, don't dude me," Kyle said as he gave her a disapproving look followed by a small burst of laughter. "What have you been up to? How'd finals go?"

"My finals were a joke. They were all really easy. I had one twenty page paper to write, which sucked, but whatever. I think it's all fine," Tash said rolling her eyes. "I have sooo much more to tell you."

Just before Tash could continue the waitress came over. "Do you know what you'd like or do you need another minute?" she asked as she put down a complimentary plate of bagel chips and spread.

Tash looked at Kyle and asked, "The regular?" to which he nodded. "We'll have a large order of blueberry cheese blintzes and two coffees. Thanks," Tash said as she handed the waitress the large plastic menus.

"What's up? What trouble have you gotten into?" Kyle asked as he dipped a marble rye bagel chip into the cream cheese olive spread.

Tash picked up a bagel chip and broke off a corner which she promptly threw at Kyle while laughing. "Trouble, trouble? I don't get into trouble; I'm a very good girl. You know that," she said, giggling.

"Yeah, yeah. So, what trouble have you been up to?" Kyle asked with a laugh.

Tash tossed another piece of a bagel chip at him but it flew past his shoulder. "Awe... sucker," he said, now hysterical. The man in the booth behind Kyle turned and looked at Natashya. She mouthed, "I'm sorry," and then Kyle proceeded to make funny faces at her, trying to provoke her to throw another chip.

"You're so bad," she said as the waitress dropped off two mugs of coffee.

"So," Tash said as they both poured mini creamers into their mugs, "I met someone really cool. You have to meet him."

"Does he go to NYU?" Kyle asked.

"No, my friend Lyric and I were..." Kyle cut her off, "Lyric? Lyric? You actually have a friend named Lyric?"

"Yeah, her name is Lyric," Tash said as she broke off another bagel chip piece and tossed it at him, hitting him right in the face because he was laughing so hard he forgot to move his head.

"Anyway, Lyyyyric and I were hanging out in the Village and we stopped in this used music store; she wanted to look into selling a bunch of her old shitty nineties CDs. She wants to buy this totally overpriced pair of Gucci boots on Ebay so she's trying to sell her old junk. Anyway, she started talking to the guy behind the counter, and the next thing you know we were all talking, and he ended up asking for my email address, and we hung out and he's so cute and it's been like three weeks of constant hanging out. He's awesome and you've got to meet him."

The waitress handed them their platter of blintzes with two small plates before Kyle could respond. "You all set here? Anything else I can get you?"

"We're good, thanks," Kyle said.

"These look awesome," Tash said as she started smearing a dollop of sour cream onto the tops of the blintzes.

"Yeah, I haven't had these in a while," Kyle said as he cut into a blintz and watched the blueberry cheese mixture ooze out. "Does he go to school? Is he older?"

"He's a musician. He plays the guitar, and he's only like a few years older than me, so it's fine," Tash said as she put a big forkful of blintz into her mouth.

"Your parents aren't gonna be happy that you're dating some random guy that works at a CD store. Good luck telling them that one," Kyle said with a smirk.

"Oh it's fine. Don't take it so seriously. Besides, why do they need to know, right?" she said as she laughed. "He's having a New Year's Eve party at his place, come with me so you can meet him. He lives in Brooklyn."

"I thought you were going home."

"Yeah, I am, but I told my parents that I need to come back December 30th for a winter session seminar. What do you say, will you come with me? You can bring Sam if you want."

"Sam's going on a cruise with his mother and her boyfriend."

"Uh, poor Sam. That sounds heinous," Tash said with a wince. "So, will you come?"

"Yeah, sure, I'll go."

"Thanks, it'll be great. So what's going on with you?" Tash asked as she loaded her fork with another bite of blintz.

"Same old, same old." For the next few minutes Kyle and Tash just ate and then, seemingly out of the blue and without looking up from his plate Kyle said, "My grandfather was in an accident. Did you hear?"

"No, no I haven't heard anything. Gee I'm really sorry. Is he ok?"

"I don't really know. My mom doesn't like to talk about it," Kyle said, still looking down.

"You don't really know your grandfather, do you?" Tash asked.

"No. Never met him."

"Crazy."

"Yeah. My mom's pretty upset, I heard her on the phone this morning talking to my aunt. She hasn't gone to visit or anything though."

"It's probably depressing for her," Tash said. Then she balanced her fork on the edge of her plate, looked straight at Kyle who looked up at her, and in a lowered voice said, "Look, a long time ago my parents told me that like your mom's family is like trailer park or something. I don't know if it's true, but…"

Trying to spare Tash from coming up with a way to finish the sentence Kyle interjected with "Yeah, I know. I think she's embarrassed by them or something. Let's talk about something else, I didn't mean to be a total downer." Kyle looked back down at his plate and took a large bite.

"Ok, sure," Tash said picking up her fork. "I need some more of this shitty coffee. Where's the waitress?"

CHAPTER 10

After spending the rest of the weekend on her couch, watching TV, napping, and drinking, all while wearing her Old Navy pants and a ratty old gray sweatshirt, Prilly managed to pull herself together to go to work Monday morning. She spent the next couple of days focusing entirely on work. She was able to block everything else out of her mind by making herself emotionally numb, a skill she learned while being bullied on the playground in third grade. She shut down so she could show up. This also helped in her dealings with Janice who now appeared downright angry.

She thoroughly edited the first batch of memoir manuscripts, which Janice had been nagging her about. The more work she did, the more Janice seemed to ease up. The memoirs came in handy too; she tried to lose herself in the stories of others. One of the books was absolutely riveting. It was about a middle-aged woman, Joyce, who was married with two grown children. She was a university professor who, along with some colleagues, volunteered for a 9-11-related charity. The group involved 9-11 widows and other volunteers working to help improve the life conditions of Afghan women. Joyce ended up going on a trip to Afghanistan where she met a poor man with one leg with whom she had a three year bi-continental affair. She fell madly in love and experienced "the emotional, cultural, and intellectual journey of a lifetime." Apparently her husband never found out. Prilly was captivated.

Prilly's newfound use of work as Prozac was short-lived. Unfortunately she had put in for extended vacation time from Christmas Eve through New Year's Day. The fact was, the press virtually shut down during that week anyway. She had intended to spend the time with Pete. Much to her parent's disapproval, she had told them she wouldn't make it home for the holidays this year. After she and Pete broke up, and she knew she would be alone, she was resigned to the solitude and never told anyone that she no longer had holiday plans. She thought about trying to work

105

so she wouldn't have to blow through her vacation days but when she broached the subject with Stu he brushed her off and told her to enjoy her vacation. He noticed how tired she seemed lately and was concerned.

The morning of Christmas Eve Prilly was in her office organizing some folders to take home with her, just in case she ended up doing some work. Suddenly Janice was standing in her doorway.

"Prilly, do you have a minute?"

"Oh, hi Janice," Prilly said startled. "Sure, what's up?"

Janice walked in and stood behind the chair in front of Prilly's desk. "Do you want to sit down?" Prilly asked.

"Oh, no, I'm fine," Janice responded. Prilly thought Janice seemed odd, even for her.

"I think we should start planning ahead to the Spring launch," Janice said in a faraway voice. "This launch is important; it will set the tone for the series and I really want to be on top of things."

"Yeah, sure," Prilly said. "What do you want to plan?"

Janice rolled her eyes. "We need to plan the organization of the booth, the signage, author book signings, support staff, everything. We can't just show up with a few books; we need to make a splash."

"Absolutely," Prilly responded. "What if the books don't make it through production by then? What if they're not ready? It's an incredibly tight schedule."

"They'll make it. It'll be close but the first batch will be there, and we'll have covers and flyers for the second group; so we can promote them even without the books. We need this to go well." Janice began to turn around when Prilly realized that other than Stu they were the only people who had come in that day.

"What are you doing for Christmas?" Prilly asked. Janice didn't respond so Prilly added, "I hope you have a good vacation."

Janice turned around softly saying "thanks" before walking out.

*

An hour later Janice headed home to an empty house. Two days earlier Richard decided to take an impromptu ski trip. Janice said she was too busy to go; Richard wasn't surprised since she didn't ski.

Richard and Kyle left early that morning to head to their family house in Stowe Vermont. They would be gone for four days.

Janice was used to being alone, but on that day she felt uncharacteristically lonely. She stopped at a local grocer near her house and picked up some ready-made food from the salad bar as well as a chilled bottle of white Zinfandel. When she entered her house she dropped her work bag at the front door and headed to the kitchen to unpack the food. She opened the wine and poured a glass. She walked back through the dining room and put the wine glass down on the table. She returned to the front door and picked up her work bag, carrying it over to the table. She sat down, sipped her wine and started to work.

The next day after making her decaf Janice called her sister's cell phone to wish her a Merry Christmas. Marge was at her mother's house so she was forced to speak to her as well. She spent the rest of the day working, exercising on her bike, and watching a Christmas double feature on TV: "Miracle on 34th Street" followed by "It's a Wonderful Life." During "It's a Wonderful Life" Richard called and he and Kyle wished her a Merry Christmas. They both asked her to think about joining them the next day but she said she had too much to do and that they should have fun.

She was back in her office the next day engrossed in her work and feeling resentful of her many colleagues who had taken a vacation week.

*

By Christmas Prilly had fallen into the depression she knew was coming. She mustered up all of her energy to call her parents. She managed to have a three minute conversation without falling apart which was an accomplishment. She spent the next several days lying on her couch watching "women's television", eating take-out, drinking and fantasizing about Pete. She wondered what he was doing, if he was with someone and if he was thinking about her at all. She didn't bother to shower or check her email. She didn't even brush her hair. As the days dragged on she felt worse and worse. There was living, and there was living a life worth living.

Right now she was barely living. Over these days Pete came to represent a life that was worth living: the life she dreamt of. While usually the tricks of memory are played out over time, in this case, it was much quicker: all she could remember were the wonderful moments of music, dance and lovemaking. Nobody like him would ever make her feel that way again. Pete was a big life.

She woke up on the morning of New Year's Eve with a new resolve. She needed to try to reconnect with Pete. She needed to see if it was possible. Her life couldn't be any worse than it already was, she couldn't be any more hopeless and so she had nothing to lose.

Though it seemed like ages ago, when they were together Prilly
and Pete spoke about New Year's Eve. Prilly made sure to bring it
up as a part of her many tests of Pete's long-term commitment. He
mentioned a club he liked that hosts a big New Year's Eve bash,
and so she reserved tickets online for them for which he praised
her, which she felt more than paid for the price of admission. In the
wake of the breakup she looked into canceling only to find out the
tickets were non-refundable. Prilly often got stuck on small stuff;
almost obsessively. In this instance, while initially irked about
losing the money for the New Year's tickets, she soon became
enraged over it, with thoughts of those unused tickets cycling over
and over again in her mind the nights she couldn't fall asleep. But
with her new determination to try to reunite with Pete she suddenly
felt the universe had actually thrown her a bone by preventing her
from hastily canceling the reservation. It was serendipity.

Over the course of that day Prilly transformed from a woman on
the verge of total collapse into a laser-sharp vixen with a plan. She
planned to get herself looking as good as possible and go to the club
in the hopes Pete would be there too.

By the time Prilly left her apartment she felt great. She wore a
long, full black skirt with tulle underneath, peaking out of the
bottom. Pete pointed out the skirt in a SoHo store window display.
She went back on her own a few days later and even though it was
way out of her price range she charged it. She paired it with a tight
white sparkly tank top, black tights and high heeled black patent
leather boots. Her hair looked great, long and sleek. She went eye-
makeup heavy with dark, smoky eyeliner and only a pale lilac
shimmering lip gloss. On her way to the front door she gave herself a
final once-over in the mirror and thought to herself, "I couldn't look
better. Perfect."

After having a very hard time hailing a cab Prilly was finally on
her way. While sitting in traffic on route doubts started to creep in.

"What if he isn't there? What if I look stupid?" And worst of all: "What if he's with someone else?" Determined to see her plan through she pushed these thoughts out of her mind afraid he would be able to read them on her face.

Upon arrival at the club she saw a long line of people waiting to show their ID. Prilly got in the back. It was freezing. Over her outfit she wore only a light black trench coat and black leather gloves; she didn't wear her winter coat, scarf or hat in case she saw him outside; she didn't want to look frumpy. When it was her turn, at first the bouncer couldn't find her name on the reservation list. She started to panic but then with a second look he found her. She was in.

As soon as Prilly walked through the door she feared she had made a horrible mistake. She had never been to a club, party or anything like it alone. Suddenly she didn't know what to do with herself. As she stood for a moment trying to get her bearings the people behind her started to push past her, making her feel all the more awkward. She glanced upward and saw a blue neon sign that noted the coat-check was down the stairs directly in front of her. She headed straight down, where she then stood in a hallway with gray walls that reminded her of the cheap stucco that lined her elementary school. It was dark with blue lights hanging from the ceiling. She leaned against the right-hand wall, waiting in a long line for the coat-check. Opposite her were women in line for the restroom, which was followed by a men's room, which men entered and exited freely. The hallway was narrow and with people lined up on both sides she felt claustrophobic. She was getting warm and started to worry that her perfectly done makeup might melt. She felt conspicuous just as she had as a kid in school. After finally hanging her coat, she decided to go to the ladies room since it was right there— she wanted to check her face and waste some more time. After standing in line on the left-hand side of the hallway Prilly entered the overcrowded women's room to discover only two of the three stalls had doors. Naturally the one that opened up was the one without a door. She squeezed to the side to wait for another one. When she finally got into a stall the toilet hadn't been flushed in a while and the floor was sticky. It was hard to balance while holding her large skirt up, and she was scared the tulle would drag across the stained floor. By the time she maneuvered her way to one of the two tiny sinks to wash her hands she glanced in the foggy mirror and assessed that she didn't look as good as she did an hour ago but she still looked ok. Feeling deflated she made her way upstairs.

At the top of the stairs she found herself in the room she initially entered, but hadn't noticed. It was a large garnet-colored room with black velvet couches and chairs. It seemed to be a mood room of sorts. People were sitting and standing everywhere. To her left there was a large room with a dance floor. She peaked inside. It was loud. Techno music was blaring, and the dark room, lit only with strobe lights and blue glow-in-the-dark necklaces that many club-goers were wearing, was absolutely packed with moving bodies. She went back through the mood room to the final room. This large open space had a slightly less crowded dance floor, with gothic-style music playing. On the left side of the room there was a long packed bar. Prilly started to make her way over when through all of the other noise she heard the unmistakable sound of Pete's laughter. When he was really laughing hard it turned into a cackle, and you couldn't miss it. Her eyes zoomed to the right hand corner of the bar where Pete was sitting on a stool talking to a few people standing around him. Her blood started coursing faster and faster. She was trying to decide if she should walk right over to him or if she should just walk to the middle of the bar, pretending not to see him, until he noticed her. As she was deciding on the latter plan Pete turned and spotted her. "Hey grrrl," he shouted loudly. He looked happy to see her.

She coyly tilted her head slightly downward and smiled. She hoped he would walk over to her but instead he waved her over to him. She felt like she might throw up as she made her way. As she approached the small group, Pete, better looking than she had remembered, jumped off his stool and hugged her. "You look beautiful," he whispered, his warm breath imprinted on her ear.

As he pulled away he said, "Prilly, this is Jay, Lacey, Kim, and you remember Veronica."

She smiled and nodded. "I was on my way to get a drink," Prilly nervously said, to which Pete responded, "Allow me my dear," in his sexiest voice. She had never met anyone more charming. He turned to the bartender a few feet away and asked for a red wine. A few moments later he handed Prilly the wine. His friend Jay said, "Pete, we're going to dance; are you coming?" Prilly held her breath in anticipation. "No, you go ahead. I'll catch up with you."

As the group walked away Pete turned to Prilly, he leaned in and said, "It's too loud here, let's go find a nice spot to sit and talk."

"Ok."

He grabbed his cranberry colored drink off of the bar with one hand and took Prilly's hand with the other. She tried not to spill her wine as they made their way through the crowd to the mood room up front. He looked around the room; there wasn't anywhere to sit. Just before he was going to say something he saw a couple of people get off of a couch in the far corner of the room. "Let's go girl," he said as he hurriedly walked over, still grasping her hand.

They sat down on the small couch and he looked her directly in her eyes. "I'm glad you came. I was hoping to see you here. You look wonderful."

Prilly smiled and looked down. "You look great too."

He slipped his hand on her cheek and she raised her head. He kissed her softly, and then made a beautiful close-mouthed smile.

"So, how have you been girl?" he asked before taking a swig of his drink.

"Ok. What about you?" she asked, also taking a sip of her wine.

"Ah, you know. Chasing the muse." Then he paused, looked down, and then right back into her eyes. "I've thought about you a lot. I've missed you."

"Me too." She didn't think she could be any happier. Her fears subsided. She was right to have gone, and for once in her life her courage was being rewarded.

Flooded with things she wanted to say to him but determined to hold onto them tightly, she felt a crack in her armor. Just as she was about to let something slip, she realized they were not alone.

"Oh, hey," Pete said. Veronica, dressed head to toe in black, was standing over them.

"Didn't mean to interrupt. Pete, just wanted to tell you that we're heading into the other room for a bit if you come looking for us."

"Ok, thanks. We have some catching up to do but we'll find you all later."

At first Prilly was thrilled-- this time Pete wanted to be with her. But then she saw the look on Veronica's face. Veronica was pissed off.

As Veronica walked off, Prilly took a big gulp of her wine. Pete gently said, "Put that down," and when she did, he took her hands in his and whispered. "Hey you, I really did miss you."

"Me too," she said. "I'm sorry if I've crashed in on your New Year's plans."

He shrugged his shoulders and smiled. "That's ok. I'm glad you're here."

"I hope your friends don't mind," Prilly said quizzically.

He shrugged again.

"Veronica seemed annoyed."

"No, she's cool." Pete said. "So my girl, what have you been up to?"

And with that they began talking about work, music, art and how much they had thought about each other. Nearly an hour later their drinks were empty. "Hey, let's get a refill," Pete said.

"Sure."

They made their way back into the large gothic room, to the bar where they had first seen each other. Pete's friends were back at the bar hanging out. "Let's join them," he said as he started to head in that direction. "Ok," she said, feeling exhilarated.

They spent the next twenty minutes drinking and hearing about the group's misadventures on the techno dance floor. Prilly would have been having a great time but she kept sensing bad vibes coming from Veronica. It began to gnaw at her. She did her best to ignore it.

Then Veronica leaned over to Pete and said, "Hey buddy, I need to talk to you," loud enough for Prilly to hear.

"Sure." He then turned to Prilly and said, "Don't go anywhere. I'll be back in a jiffy. Go have a dance."

Prilly watched as he and Veronica exited the room. Jay asked if she wanted to dance. "No thanks, I'm good," she said before sipping her wine. With that Jay and Lacey went to dance and Kim wandered off. Prilly was left just standing there, but only for a few minutes. When Pete returned he was alone.

"Hey girl, sorry about that."

"It's ok. Is everything alright? Where's Veronica?" Prilly asked.

"She needed some air, went for a smoke outside I think. She'll be back," Pete said while looking over at his friends on the dance floor.

"Pete, is there something going on with you two? Are you on a date or something?"

Pete looked at Prilly and smiled. "No, no, it's not a date at all. We all came together as friends."

"Oh, cuz she seemed kinda upset. She was glaring at me too."

"What?" Pete hollered. The music was loud and it was hard to hear.

Prilly leaned in and asked, "Can we go back into the other room?"

"Sure. Let's go."

They walked back into the front room to discover there weren't any free seats. They leaned against a wall and Pete asked, "What were you saying before? I couldn't hear you."

"I was just saying that Veronica seemed to be giving me weird looks, and I was just wondering what was up."

"She's just protective of me, that's all."

Prilly was puzzled. "Protective of you, from me? Why? I don't understand."

"I was kinda messed up when we stopped seeing each other. She doesn't want me to get hurt, that's all."

Prilly was ecstatic to learn that Pete had been so seriously impacted by the break-up. It wasn't just her. What she thought they had was in fact real. Then Pete made a funny face and said, "There may be a bit of jealousy there too."

Suddenly Prilly's runaway happiness hit a wall. "Jealous; why?" She paused and asked, "Does she have a thing for you?"

"Oh, I don't know," he said in a blasé tone. "We slept together a couple of times, just like a friend thing with no strings, but I think she might want more."

"I thought you were just friends," Prilly quickly said, trying to hide her shock.

"We are. It was just a friends with benefits kind of thing. Scratch the itch. You know how it is."

"When? When was it?" Prilly demanded.

"What does it matter?"

"I just want to know," Prilly responded.

"A couple of times after we broke up. Didn't mean anything, was just trying to get past you. It was more about missing you than anything else."

With those words Prilly's heart imploded. While she had been devastated, he had been sleeping someone who looked like a teenager. It was too much to handle.

"I can't believe it. I've made such an awful mistake," she frantically said as she started to leave.

Pete grabbed her shoulder. "Not this shit again. I told you it's nothing. It's you I've been thinking about." And then his tone sharpened. "Don't be stupid girl."

With those cutting words she turned around and walked straight out of the club. She knew she had left her coat and gloves but was too proud and embarrassed to go get them.

The streets were crowded and she couldn't see any empty cabs. There were bright lights and she felt turned upside down. The ground was slick and in her hysteria she stumbled several times twisting her ankles. Freezing, she spotted a small convenient store and hurried in for warmth. Desperate, she bought a $35 white

"I Love NY" sweatshirt, two sizes too big, which she pulled over her head immediately. She headed back outside in search of a taxi. After about ten minutes she got lucky. She felt like puking and had to open the cab window even though it was freezing. She made it home just before midnight. After raising the heat in her apartment to try and thaw out she took off her boots, tights and skirt and got into bed. She tried to cry but couldn't.

Lying in bed she wished she had never met him. Then she could still hope; still think something or someone big was ahead of her. And in the meantime she wouldn't really know what she was missing.

*

Kyle met up with Tash outside of her dorm at 8:00 pm on New Year's Eve. To his surprise she was standing outside waiting when he arrived. Her parents had given her some money for the holidays; so, feeling it burning a hole in her pocket, she decided they would splurge on a taxi to Brooklyn which she had wisely ordered in advance.

Tash was wearing skintight black jeans (so tight that Kyle wondered how she was able to get them on). He thought about making a comment as she got into the cab, pushing him to the other side, but decided against it. He also noticed what looked like 4 or 5 inch black patent leather high heels. He sarcastically mused to himself how much fun it would be helping her walk later when she would undoubtedly be drunk and stumbling around. She had a lot of makeup on too; her blue eyes were smoky and dark, and her lips glistened hot pink. She was wearing a long, low-cut sparkly silver top and a black motorcycle jacket that struck him as odd. He had never seen her wear it, or anything like it, before. Right after telling the driver where to go Tash started fiddling around in her hobo-style silver studded black bag.

"What are you looking for?" Kyle asked.

"Gum. But I have so much crap in here I can't find anything." She started to giggle and said, "I need one of those lights that you like tape into the inside of your bag. Have you ever seen those lights? You know, from the infomercials. They're hysterical."

Before Kyle could respond, Tash continued all the while searching through her bag. "God I love those infomercials. Don't you love them?" she asked exuberantly. "Sometimes when I can't sleep at night I watch them for hours. The stuff always starts out looking crappy but by the fourth or fifth testimonial I'm hooked! I swear! And the acting, that's the best part. It's like watching a soap opera or porn or something. At first it seems totally fake but then somehow it starts to seem believable. Did you ever notice that?"

"Yeah, it's kind of like watching wrestling. Sometimes Sam and I joke about…" but before Kyle could finish his thought "Uh Huh!" Tash pronounced as she pulled a jumbo pack of Juicy Fruit gum out of her bag. "Want a piece?" she asked as she unwrapped two pieces and shoved them in her mouth.

"No thanks," Kyle replied. "Listen, Tash, what's the deal with the party we're going to tonight?"

"What do you mean?" she asked as she zipped her bag. "I told you that the guy I am seeing is having a party with his roommate. I've met a few of their friends too. They're cool; they're like indie musician types. You'll like them."

"It's a little weird for me going when I don't know any of these guys and, and…" he paused briefly. "I want to hang together," he said turning his gaze from the cab window to Tash.

As she spit out her huge wad of gum into the wrapper and proceeded to drop it on the floor of the cab she quickly said, "Just don't worry about it. Just be yourself; it'll be fun. It's a small place; you couldn't lose me if you tried. We can totally crash there too if we want to."

Kyle turned away. He leaned his head against the door looking out the window hoping that the night wouldn't be too miserable and hoping he wouldn't end up sleeping on some guy's floor listening to him screw his cousin.

Finally they arrived. Kyle got out of the cab while Tash paid the driver. Standing on the sidewalk he could hear what sounded like hip-hop music blasting from above. It was freezing and he wished Tash would hurry. When Tash hopped out of the cab she grabbed Kyle tightly by the hand and said, "Let's go." The front door to the building had been pried open with a few bricks. As they made their way upstairs Kyle could feel the stairs themselves vibrating from the overly loud music. He wondered if all the other tenants were brain dead or out for New Years. It seemed like the kind of place where people without New Year's plans would live. The building was musty and had a foul smell. Before he could process all of this he was being led by hand into an overcrowded dark apartment that positively reeked of cigarette and pot smoke. He suspected that it had smelled that way for years and that the smell would forever linger. There were bodies everywhere and they seemed to be in motion. The small apartment itself seemed to be throbbing from the wall-to-wall people and booming music. Tash continued to pull Kyle through the crowd in the living room. She approached a closed door and flung it open. The bright lights and smell of pot hit them as, dropping Kyle's hand and flinging her arms up in the air, Tash announced, "Hey baby. I made it."

There were four or five guys crowded onto a twin bed and a couple of girls sitting on the floor on the side of the room. One of the guys put his hands out and said, "I was waiting for you. But we had to start the party without you." He then got up and walked over to Tash and Kyle.

"Hey man, how are you doin?" he asked as he put out his hand.

"Hey," Kyle said quietly.

"This is my cousin Kyle," Tash interjected.

"Well I'm Jacob, this is my room," he said as he casually waved one arm around "these are my friends and that's my stash. Ha. That's funny, dude, I just realized Tash and stash rhyme. So now I got my stash and I got my Tash," he proclaimed as he took Tash's hand and then broke out into hysterics. The guys sitting on the bed started laughing too. Turning back to Kyle Jacob said, "Hey, seriously dude. Welcome to my humble abode. Mi casa es su casa. There's beer and shit in the living room, there's party supplies in here, go crazy."

"Thanks man," Kyle said struck by how utterly unappealing this guy seemed. He was on the short side and had greasy-looking straw-colored hair. He was clearly behind on a haircut too. He was wearing light blue jeans and a totally outdated flannel shirt. In the middle of talking to Kyle he grabbed a plastic cowboy hat that had been perched on the corner of a chair and put it on his head. He proceeded to tip his hat to Tash and say, "You look mighty hot little girl." All and all, Kyle thought he seemed like a loser. He was glad he put the hat on though, if only to reduce the chances of any lice jumping off of his head and onto someone else's.

"Let's hang in here for a while, okay?" Tash said to Kyle. Kyle nodded as she and Jacob plopped onto the bed. The other people on the bed started to move over to make room for them. "You come too," Tash said to Kyle while giving him an encouraging look. "I'm cool," he said as he grabbed the chair where Jacob's hat had been, turned it around to face the group, and sat down.

"Dude, give Natashya some of that," Jacob said to the guy to his left who was holding a joint. The guy passed it to Jacob, and Natashya put her hand out but Jacob said "uh uh" as he shook his head and smiled at her. Then he took a big drag, sucking it in deeply, and with his free hand he grabbed the back of Tash's head and pulled her mouth to his and proceeded to blow the smoke into her mouth. The other guys on the couch passed juvenile looks back and forth and smiled. Tash inhaled deeply holding the smoke down while offering a closed grin. Then she started to giggle letting the smoke free. They smiled at each other, and then Jacob turned toward Kyle holding the joint outward. "Here you go man."

"No thanks, I'm good," Kyle said.

"Suit yourself dude," Jacob replied as he passed the joint back to the guy who had it before him.

"Kyle's a straight edge," Tash said in between giggles.

"Hey, that's cool. To each their own you know," Jacob said.

Over the next hour or so they talked a little about music (including how they were all too lazy to go and tell the people in the other room to turn it down), movies (mostly movies aimed at adolescent boys) and even politics (but this conversation was painfully limited). The major attraction of the room was the endless pot supply. After about an hour of this Jacob pulled a sandwich size Ziploc bag out of his front jean pocket. It was filled with little pills. "Come on baby, let's feel good," he said to Tash. He started passing them around the room and everybody took one; everyone except for Kyle.

Tash leaned forward toward Kyle and said, "They're just X, Kye. They make you feel reeeeeally good. It's awesome. You should try one. It's New Years."

"Nah, I don't think so. I'm good," Kyle said with one shake of his head.

"Suit yourself," Tash said as Jacob popped one into her open mouth.

"Didn't know you were doin that stuff," Kyle remarked with a serious look.

"Well I'm a woman of mystery," Tash said seductively before laughing like a child.

The night continued to drag on for Kyle. He was infinitely bored, and at this point Tash was leaning onto Jacob who was holding her, rubbing her ass in a circular motion. Between that and the incredible swirl of smoke in the almost entirely unventilated room Kyle finally got up and said, "I'm gonna grab a drink in the other room, check out the music." Tash barely noticed him leave but as he walked out the door Jacob hollered, "Have fun man, I'll take good care of Natashya."

Kyle left the room mortified for Tash whom he heard giggling as someone kicked the door shut. Finding himself standing in a dark and overcrowded room full of strangers and blaring music he couldn't stand, Kyle knew all too well that he had made a horrible mistake. He made his way to the kitchen area which was a mess. It was overloaded with open bottles of hard liquor and open bags of corn ships and Doritos that looked mostly empty, many with spilled half broken chips on the counter. The kitchen sink was overflowing with beer cans floating in melting ice. There were dirty red plastic cups everywhere. Kyle searched for a clean cup and settled for what looked like the cleanest cup. In search of something non-alcoholic he opened the fridge and instinctively threw his head back in horror at the revolting smell. He saw several half-empty bottles of Mountain Dew on the refrigerator door. He pulled one out and poured a cup. The smoke was killing his throat and he needed to drink. He chugged it down and refilled his cup before returning the bottle to the refrigerator.

He surveyed the room but couldn't see anywhere to sit or anyone he wanted to talk to. He stood by the kitchen counter and slowly drank his second cup of flat soda. He then started to look for a bathroom. He saw a closed door that he assumed was the bathroom. With the music so loud that people on the street could hear it he didn't see any point knocking; so he just twisted the knob and gently opened the door. It was a very small bedroom of sorts with a guy lying on a small couch, wearing large '80s style headphones, with his eyes shut. As Kyle went to close the door the guy looked over at him. "Hey, sorry man, just looking for the bathroom." Kyle stood there for a minute waiting for a response but the guy didn't say anything. "Sorry man," Kyle said again as he pulled the door shut.

After going to the bathroom Kyle was able to grab a seat on the couch when somebody got up to go get a beer. For most of the night he sat there alone occasionally chatting with whoever would sit down next to him. When people started to leave around 2:00 am and someone finally turned the music off he hoped Tash would emerge from Jacob's room. He hated the thought of having to go get her. He dreaded seeing whatever state she was in by this point. Just as he was about to get up and go check on her Tash stumbled out of the room and made her way to the bathroom. Five minutes later she came out of the bathroom and was heading back towards Jacob's room. Kyle jumped up and darted over to her. "Hey. What's up? Are you almost ready to go?"

"Oh, Kyle. I'm so glad you're still here. I didn't know if you had left," she said with her eyes swirling. Her eye makeup was smudged and her cheeks were bright red. She hugged him.

"I wouldn't leave you, you know that. You're a mess; let's get you out of here," Kyle said.

"No, I'm good. I'm reeeally good. I wanna crash here. I told you I wanted to crash here, remember. You can stay too, ok?"

"Come on, I'll take you to my place and put you in the spare room. We can go out for blintzes in the morning," Kyle rebutted.

"Naw, that's ok. I'm gonna crash here. But you can totally go home if you want to. I'm fine," Tash said.

Even though he realized she had probably stayed there many times before and that it probably didn't matter whether he was there or not, and even though he detested the thought of spending the night in that rat hole, there was no way he was leaving her there. Not in that condition and with those people.

He sighed and said, "I'll stay too."

"Oh, you're the best," Tash said as she grabbed him for a tighter hug, half falling onto him. We can still do blintzes in the morning, ok?" she slurred.

"Uh huh," Kyle said with a nod. "Where should I sleep?"

"Stay here, I'll find out."

With that Tash went back into Jacob's room. Kyle waited for about 10 minutes before Jacob came out holding a pillow. "Dude, when everyone gets outta here you can crash on the couch. There's a blanket thingie on the back of the couch you can use. Ok, dude? You all set?"

"Yeah, I'm all set," Kyle said wondering how wasted Jacob was.

Kyle spent the next hour and a half sitting on the couch with a stained pillow on his lap waiting for everyone to leave. Eventually, although there were still a handful of people mulling around the apartment, the couch was empty. Exhausted, Kyle took the pillow with cigarette burns in it and lied down. He never saw whatever blanket Jacob had been talking about so he took off his coat and draped it over his chest.

*

The next morning Kyle slowly woke up to the sound of someone stirring nearby. He opened his eyes just a little bit and was overcome by the sunlight pouring into the room. He closed his eyes and rubbed the crusty sleep out of the corners. He slowly opened them again, just a crack. He saw a guy standing in the kitchen pouring cereal into a bowl. It was the same guy that had been lying alone in that room the night before. Kyle watched him with his eyes opened only slightly. The guy opened the refrigerator and took out a carton of milk. He took a sniff and then poured some into his cereal bowl. As he fished around in a drawer presumably to get a spoon, Kyle became distracted by another noise. His eyes, opened merely a crack, veered to the right where he saw Jacob's bedroom door open and a guy, wearing only boxer shorts, walk out of the room and go into another bedroom, shutting the door behind him. His half-opened eyes quickly darted back to the left but the mysterious man was now on his way back into his room with his cereal bowl in hand. Kyle continued to lie on the couch awake but with his eyes shut for about an hour and a half until Tash emerged from Jacob's bedroom. He pretended to be asleep as she stumbled out of the room wearing an oversized Rolling Stones T-shirt that he assumed she borrowed from Jacob. Tash went straight to the bathroom. Ten minutes later she was tiptoeing back to Jacob's room when Kyle outstretched his arms and made a noise as if he was just waking up.

"Oh, hey. Sorry. Didn't mean to wake you up," Tash said.

"No worries," he moaned. "I'm sure it's time to get up anyway." Kyle started to sit up as he asked, "Where's Jacob?"

"Oh, he's still sleepin'. Knowing him he could sleep for half the day. He really partied last night."

Tash walked over to the couch and sat down next to Kyle. Her shoulders were hunched over like she was cold. Kyle put his coat on her bare legs. "Thanks," she said. She looked awful. Her thick black eyeliner was now smeared all around her eyes making her look like a raccoon staring at rapidly approaching car headlights.

"You hungry?" Kyle asked.

"Nah, not really. I'm just super tired. I only got up because I was bursting and had to pee. You wanna get out of here?"

"Sure."

"I just have to get dressed. I'll be right back." With that Tash got up and went into Jacob's room. Kyle went and used the bathroom, and when he came out Tash was waiting there dressed and wearing black sunglasses. Kyle grabbed his coat and they headed outside. Tash leaned against the building smoking cigarettes while Kyle tried to get a cab (which took nearly 20 minutes).

They sat in silence for the first few minutes of the cab ride and then, feeling very uncomfortable, Kyle said, "Last night I was looking for the bathroom and accidentally walked in on this guy lying alone in a room. I saw him again getting cereal this morning. Do you know who that guy is and why he stayed alone in his room all night?"

"Oh, that's Jacob's loser brother. Melvyn, or Melville, or Mel-something. He's a freak. Jacob just lets him crash there because he'd be like homeless otherwise. He's a total dweeb," Tash said while leaning against the car door and looking in Kyle's direction (still with her dark sunglasses making it difficult to see if her eyes were in fact open).

"Oh. I kind of felt badly for him. It was really loud there last night."

"Don't feel bad for him. He's a loser. He's lucky to be able to stay there at all," Tash quipped back.

Kyle was quiet for a minute, thinking about what to say next. After a moment passed he asked, "So who else lives there? How many roommates does Jacob have?"

"You're full of questions today," Tash groaned. Before Kyle could respond she continued, "He has one roommate, Jeremy, plus his loser brother who stays there; but he's not really a roommate exactly."

Knowing full-well that Jeremy must have been the guy that came out from Jacob's bedroom nearly naked this morning Kyle asked, "Oh, did I meet Jeremy last night?"

"Yeah, he was one of the guys in Jacob's room, on the couch. He's kind of a prick." She paused and then said, "I'm super fried; can we just chill the rest of the way?"

"Yeah, sure," Kyle responded. It seemed like a perfect time to stop talking anyway.

They arrived at Tash's dorm first. When they pulled up to the curb she started going through her bag. She was fumbling around unable to find her money. She dumped the contents of the bag onto the backseat of the cab. Her money wasn't there. As she started to scoop everything back into her bag she said, "Hey, Kyle I…" but he cut her off and said, "Don't worry, I got it."

"I don't know what happened to my cash. Maybe it fell out of my bag or something. Sorry," she said unconvincingly as she leaned in and gave him a half-hearted hug.

As she stepped out of the cab Kyle leaned towards her door and said, "Blintzes another time."

"Yeah, sure. See ya."

When the taxi arrived at Kyle's house he asked the driver to please wait while he ran in to grab some money. He walked into the house leaving the front door ajar while he hurried to his room for the cash. Janice was sitting at the dining room table wearing a long silk robe and working on her laptop. She hollered, "You left the door open."

Before she could either get up to close the door or ask Kyle to do it, he was coming back down the stairs and racing out the door. A moment later he came back into the house. "Hey Mom. Sorry about that. I didn't have enough money for the cab driver."

"Cabs are a rip-off. That's the great thing about the city, the subway," Janice said quietly, without looking up from her computer.

"Yeah, I know," he said as he started to head back up to his room. From halfway up the stairs he said, "Hey Mom, Happy New Year."

"You too, Honey."

Kyle went into his room, flung his shoes off and plopped down on his bed. He grabbed his cell phone from his nightstand. There was a text from Sam saying Happy New Year and complaining about the trip he was on. Kyle responded: "Back at you bro. That's nothin. I got stuck in Brooklyn with Tash. She's into a bad scene. Will tell u later." Although he would tell Sam all about the atrocious party, and how Tash was smoking up and popping pills, he would never mention the second guy that came out of Jacob's room to anyone.

Lying on his bed he kept thinking about how Tash seemed to be spiraling downward. Then he started to think about how much it irked him when Jacob called her Tash instead of Natashya. He had never heard anyone else call her that, not even her roommate.

Prilly pulled herself out of bed at noon on New Year's Day only because she was sweating; still wearing the oversized sweatshirt she bought the night before. She also had to pee badly. She actually thought about just going in the bed but knew she would regret it shortly thereafter. She slowly walked to the bathroom and while sitting on the toilet she pulled the sweatshirt over her head and threw it on the floor in the corner behind the door. She left the bathroom without flushing the toilet or washing her hands. Shoulders slumped, she shuffled back into her room where she opened her dresser drawer and pulled out an old pair of gray yoga pants and a matching long-sleeved cotton shirt. She changed and got back into bed. She forced herself to go back to sleep. Two hours later she woke up with a headache. She took four Advil and made a pot of coffee. She stood in the kitchen as the coffee brewed and stared at her answering machine. There weren't any messages. She took a cup of coffee and a box of crackers and walked into the living room. She sat on her couch flipping through stations looking for something to watch. There wasn't much on because of the holiday. All of the things that usually comforted her, like movies of the week, seemed to be mocking her. She settled on a station that showed infomercials all day long. Vacant and numb she sat and watched for hours only occasionally getting up to get something to snack on or to go to the bathroom. With New Year's Day falling on a Thursday she had until Monday to pull herself together before leaving her apartment and returning to work. She couldn't imagine ever going anywhere again. She felt dead. She had never felt so empty, so worthless and so lifeless. She spent the next few days in her apartment watching TV, sleeping, eating frozen dinners and forcing herself not to call Pete. She told herself over and over again that she could never call him again.

*

Janice's alarm rang at 5:00 am the Monday after New Year's. She sprung from bed and got ready for work selecting her favorite gray pencil skirt, white button-down shirt and a long black cashmere cardigan. She was in her office before 7:00.

Prilly arrived in her office at 9:10. She had psyched herself up the night before, telling herself that things would somehow get better if she could manage to get up in the morning, take a shower and get herself to work. She made it her mission to be on time but due to a subway delay she still managed to be 10 minutes late. As she hurried into her office, throwing her work bag on the floor and flopping down in her chair, Janice appeared at her office door. She hadn't even been able to turn her computer on. "Did you hear?" Janice asked.

"Oh, hi Janice," Prilly nervously said as she pressed the power button on her computer. She was convinced that everyone could suddenly see what a worthless mess she was.

"Did you hear?" Janice repeated, this time agitated.

"Oh, I'm sorry. Uh, did I hear what?" Prilly asked as she typed her password into her email login screen.

"Charles Pruit committed suicide on New Year's Eve," Janice said matter-of-factly.

Prilly stopped all bodily motion, looked up from her computer screen, and with trembling fingers softly asked, "What? What did you say?"

"Charles Pruit committed suicide. Jumped out of his apartment window or something on New Year's Eve. Hell Prilly it's been all over the news and Stuart sent out an email days ago." She then snidely finished with, "Where have you been?"

In shock, Prilly couldn't think of what to say.

"He was one of your authors, right?" Didn't you reject his latest book or something?" Janice asked, knowing all too well the answers to these questions.

"Oh my God. Yeah, yeah, Stuart didn't want to go with it," Prilly muttered, still searching for coherent words.

"Well it's not your fault. He must have been a nut," Janice said right before she turned around and walked away.

Prilly just sat there. Not a minute later her computer beeped indicating the delivery of a new email. It was from Janice and read:

Prilly: We need to get moving with our series. I have been working for several days and I have been here since early this morning. You need to pull your weight. I want to see your notes by the end of the day. I will be sending my notes attached to several forthcoming emails. J.

Prilly opened her desk drawer, pulled out her bottle of Advil, and then just sat with it in her hands as if unable to muster up the energy to open it. She put her head down on her desk.

A few minutes later she heard Stuart's voice: "Hey, are you ok there?"

Prilly popped up, "Oh Stuart, I'm sorry I..."

"It's all right. I know," he said as he walked into her office, shutting the door behind him, and sitting down across from her. "I know how hard this must be for you but honestly Prilly, the guy must have been pretty messed up. It's got nothing to do with you or with us. He was depressed, chronically depressed. He needed help."

"Yeah. I'm sure you're right," Prilly responded, not knowing what to say but hoping Stuart, though always nice to her, would leave so she could be alone.

They sat for a moment in an uncomfortable silence. Then Stuart said, "Listen, Prilly, I realize this might be tough for you. If you're really troubled by it you might want to talk to someone about it. I can get a name for you."

She was startled by his suggestion and wanted to take the spotlight off of her emotional state. "I appreciate your concern; thank you. But I'm really fine. I barely knew him," she said in a way that she hoped made her sound together even though she was quite rattled. With decades on her, Stuart in some ways thought of Prilly as a kid. He also liked her, and so he felt badly for her.

"Well you know where to find me if I can be of any help," he said as he stood up and pushed his chair back.

When he reached the door he turned back and said, "By the way, Happy New Year. Hope you had a good break. Janice said you two are working on some exciting stuff. Look forward to catching up on it all."

"Thanks Stu. Uh Happy New Year to you too," Prilly managed to get out as he was walking away.

She sat for a moment until she realized that she was still clutching the bottle of Advil. She opened her desk drawer and dropped the bottle, never having opened it. She started to think about Charles. She felt guilty. In her heart of hearts she knew that the rejection had at least been a part of it. She even understood. Then she started to think about Pete, about the last few days, and about how broken she was. A part of her envied Charles.

Her thoughts were interrupted by another beep from her computer. It was another new e-mail from Janice that read:

P: My notes are attached. More forthcoming. J.

Prilly's inbox had 79 new messages, not including those from Janice. She knew she needed to get to work and so she did.

She managed to work all day, catching up on emails and making final editorial notes on the memoir manuscripts. At 6:15 Janice came to her office and suggested they have a working lunch together the next day to review where they are and what they need to accomplish to make Trade Launch. Prilly agreed and Janice told her to make a 12:00 o'clock reservation at Nicos, an Italian restaurant two blocks from their office. Janice would meet her there. Prilly didn't have the energy to question how it was that Janice was always able to turn her into a secretary, so she just said "Sure, no problem."

"I'm glad to see you're still here," Janice remarked before turning her back and saying, "See you tomorrow."

Prilly was about to pack up and leave but now feeling self-conscious she spent another half an hour in her office, although she didn't get anything done.

When she got home she changed into her comfy clothes, made a grilled cheese sandwich, poured a glass of red wine and headed straight to her computer. She had waited all day to read the news reports about Charles. Worried her Internet usage might be monitored at work, she waited until she was home. While her computer was booting up she took a few bites of her sandwich and then set it aside. As soon as she typed "Charles Pruit" into Google a slew of newspaper articles and YouTube news clips popped up. She sat reading, watching and drinking for two hours, watching some clips over and over again.

She was able to picture what had happened that night. He was alone in his tiny studio apartment. There were stacks of books and a desk with a computer on it. He was wearing a white undershirt and pajama pants with a robe. He was watching the New Year's Eve festivities around the world on his old television perched on top of a small plastic TV stand. He was drinking Jack Daniels. He kept refilling his glass. He had been planning this for a while. Maybe in those final hours he hoped for a miracle; some great change to come and sweep over the defeat. But he was alone. At 11:30 pm he took a swig out of his glass and dropped it on the floor beside his chair. He walked over to the one window in his apartment, opened it and climbed out onto the fire escape. Without hesitation, he jumped. Prilly wondered if he had intended to wait for midnight but just couldn't make it.

From the various reports, she was able to put together the facts of his life in such a way that it all made perfect sense to her. Charles was 48 years old and had never been married and didn't have children. From what she could tell he hadn't had anyone special in his life. He was an only child and was survived by his 74 year old mother who lived in New Haven, Connecticut. Many of his colleagues and students were interviewed for various news stories. They all said it was surprising but that he was a quiet man who kept to himself. Several reporters asked his department chairperson if it was true that he had been denied a promotion recently. The chairperson had no comment. The President of the university made a statement "expressing deep sympathy for his mother" and "confidence that our community will rebound from this terrible tragedy." Prilly thought it was unspeakably sad that a 48 year old man had only left behind his mother. There may be no one else grieving for him. She felt a kinship with him. She also felt increasingly guilty.

She lay in bed for more than an hour that night before falling asleep. At first she was thinking about how desolate and disappointed by life Charles must have been. He couldn't escape the smallness of it all. Then she started thinking that's how she would end up. "Hell, that's how I've already ended up," she muttered to herself. She started to think about how lonely she had been for so long and how connected she felt with Pete. She couldn't understand how she could love someone so much who cared so little for her. Then she started to wonder if maybe he did love her and that she had caused all of this. She had shown him that she didn't deserve him. He might not have figured it out until he was so in love that it wouldn't have mattered, but she revealed herself to him. And now she was utterly alone again, more alone then she could have imagined. If not for her newfound posthumous bond with Charles, she wouldn't have anyone.

*

The next day Prilly arrived at the restaurant at 11:55 am. Consumed with thoughts of Pete and Charles she barely slept the night before and was frazzled from a long morning in the office trying to organize all of her notes for the memoir series before the dreaded lunch meeting. As she was giving her name to the host she spotted Janice already waiting at a table diagonally across the restaurant. She told the host she was "all set" and started walking towards Janice who was looking down and writing. As she approached the table Janice looked up and said, "Oh, there you are," as if Prilly was late. "Oh, I'm sorry if I kept you waiting," Prilly said, wondering if in fact she was somehow late. Janice's first move was always the same, throwing her opponent off balance. Janice was sitting on the booth side of a table for four. She had a yellow legal pad and pen in front of her and a stack of manila folders to her right. Prilly sat in a chair opposite her and placed her work on the chair beside her. There was a long rectangular mirror running the length of the wall behind Janice. Prilly immediately found herself distracted by it; vacillating from looking directly at Janice to looking just beyond her at her own reflection. Prilly thought she looked terrible. "So how are you doing?" Prilly asked, as she placed her napkin on her lap.

"Oh you know, busy busy. I'm always madly busy. I always take so much on. I think we should start working because there's a lot to get through. Do you know what you're having for lunch? When the waiter comes I think we should order right away."

"Oh, um I haven't looked yet. What are you having?" Prilly asked as she opened her menu.

"The ravioli special," Janice said.

"Oh, that sounds good. I'll have that too," Prilly said, closing her menu just as soon as she had opened it. She then pulled a notebook and pen out of her bag right as the waiter walked over and asked if they wanted to order a drink. Janice replied, "We're ready to order lunch. I will have a club soda with a piece of lime and the ravioli."

"I'll have the ravioli as well and a Diet Coke please," Prilly said, looking up at the waiter.

"Very good. I'll bring some bread over," he said as he reached to take their menus.

"Well, let's get started," Janice suggested.

They spent the next hour and a half reviewing their notes on the memoirs they had received to date. They talked about final editing, marketing, soliciting endorsements for the books and many other issues. Janice did most of the talking, and Prilly did most of the note-taking; although Prilly felt a strange synergy working with her. They bounced ideas off of each other well and seemed to have an impressive batch of books lined up as well as an innovative marketing strategy. They continued talking through their wonderful meal of spinach and ricotta-filled ravioli in a chunky tomato sauce. Prilly hadn't eaten a decent meal in weeks and realized she was starving for nourishment. It was so good that she used a piece of Italian bread to soak up the remaining sauce in her bowl but felt awkward when Janice shot her a disapproving look.

As they were wrapping up their work the waiter came over and asked if he could get them anything else. Janice ordered a decaf cappuccino; so Prilly said, "That sounds good, I'll have one too, regular though please."

"So, I think we're in pretty good shape here. We'll just need to hustle and get on the production team to get these books out," Janice said as she started to put her manila folders back into her Louis Vuitton briefcase.

"Yeah, I think so too. This is going to be a great line. I will get on that list of reviewers for commentary as soon as we get back to the office," Prilly said as she too started to put her pad and pen into her bag.

At that point the waiter walked over and handed them their cappuccinos accompanied by two pieces of amaretto biscotti. Janice picked up one of the pieces of biscotti and started dunking it into her cappuccino. "I hope this is decaf. You never know," she said before breaking out into a high-pitched laugh.

Prilly smiled and feigned a quick laugh thinking how she would hate to see Janice over-caffeinated. She then dropped two lumps of sugar into her cappuccino and started to stir it. "So," Janice said, "What's been going on with you?" she asked just before taking the last bite of her biscotti.

"Oh, not much. You know, nothing really new," Prilly said while playing with the biscotti in her hand. Janice stared at Prilly, without expression or waiver. Prilly dunked her biscotti into her cappuccino and, looking down at it said, "It's been kind of a tough time. I broke up with someone." She took a bite of the soggy biscotti. It felt surprisingly good to say it out loud. If naming something makes it real Prilly needed to take something that was the most real thing in her life and make it known in a way she could control. It somehow made her feel less crazy. Although she hadn't had any intention of talking about anything personal with Janice, certainly not Pete, it felt completely natural coming out of her mouth. "The holidays were kind of tough. You know how New Year's is, and, and I had thought we would be together."

As she swallowed the mushy cookie Janice responded with, "Oh, I'm sorry to hear that. What happened?"

"Well," she said before pausing to take a sip of her cappuccino, "I don't really know. I think he had commitment issues."

"Oh, I see," Janice said.

"He's very free-spirited. He's an artist. He's amazingly talented. And he has that free-spirited artist mentality, you know? I just didn't know if I could handle it." Prilly consciously stopped to sip her drink, wanting to know what Janice would say.

"Those artist-types are tough," Janice said, and then she started to laugh. Prilly laughed too. Then Janice returned to her stern face, looking right at Prilly. "Was it a serious relationship?" she asked.

"Yes. It was. I thought it was it. I thought he was the one." Janice offered a sympathetic look and Prilly couldn't believe how easy it was to tell her all of this.

"If they're not ready, they're not ready. If the most they can offer is less than the minimum you're willing to accept than there's no point. Sometimes it's better to cut your losses and move on. Women who try to change them only end up miserable. They waste a lot of time, and tell me what do they have to show for it? What?" she repeated, again breaking out into cackling laughter. "Sometimes these things are for the best. You should focus on your career. Then you'll have something to show for yourself," Janice said firmly.

Prilly was a life-long romantic. She believed in soul mates, great loves and, above all, big lives. But she also didn't think everyone got to have all of those things. Being in the middle, her chances were slim. She tried to envision a life worth living without them, without him. She realized that there was no way Janice shared her romantic disposition and so she couldn't really understand her pain, and Prilly wasn't about to tell her. Yet she wondered if there was something to learn from someone who had made career her priority but still wasn't alone, still had a family, or so it seemed at least.

"Thanks. I'm sure you're right. I'm going to try and focus on work and on myself. It's just hard. It's a let down."

"Sometimes the best thing we can do is to pick ourselves up and that's what you've got to do. Trust me Prilly, at the end of the day what do you want to have to show for yourself? And this memoir series is a big opportunity for you. You don't want to blow it. You can't afford to be distracted," Janice said sternly. "We both need to do our part."

"Oh, of course," Prilly said, realizing the tenor of the conversation had slipped from under her. "Absolutely, I won't be distracted. I'm actually very glad to have the work to focus on." Although Prilly was just saying it because she felt she had to, she also did feel good to have a project that demanded her attention.

"Stuart is expecting a lot from us. I promised him the sun and the moon," Janice said, again starting to laugh. "So now we have to deliver."

"Absolutely. I think we're in really good shape. I feel good about it," Prilly replied with newfound confidence.

"There's a lot of work ahead but I think we'll get there. We'll pull it off," Janice said with an uncharacteristic smile.

"So what about you? How were your holidays?" Prilly asked.

"Oh well, they were fine. My husband and son are doing really well. We just decided to stay around here this year because my husband and I are both so busy with work. He has a very demanding career too, and it never lets up," Janice said before sipping her cappuccino.

"Sometimes it's nice to stay at home and catch up on things," Prilly replied.

And with that Janice said, "Are you ready? I think we need to get back to the office. We have an action plan now."

The next five weeks Prilly followed a strict routine as if her life depended on it. She was in the office every day by 8:30. Janice usually arrived by 8:00 if not earlier and often started Prilly's day by popping unannounced into her office to review her latest ideas. Prilly worked hard, both on her considerable normal responsibilities and, even more so, on the memoir series. She was determined to stay focused while at the office. There were long-circulating rumors that the press was in trouble and cuts may be coming; rumors Janice was all too eager to spread. With the economy in the crapper and several years of declining book sales across the country in a world gone digital, Prilly took Janice's warnings more seriously than usual. Especially since she had been living off of credit cards for years as it was, rotating debt from one low-interest card to another, for fees that she chose to "think about later," and she was just barely managing to keep all of those balls in the air. She needed her job. Prilly also began to appreciate her newfound working relationship with Janice. Most days they met several times in their offices in addition to the countless e-mails that Janice sent her. On several occasions they returned to Nicos for lunch meetings. Janice always had the ravioli, and Prilly usually did too. On other occasions they had sandwiches delivered and ate in Prilly's office. Despite the difficulties Prilly still encountered working with Janice (incessant e-mailing, last-minute changes and being "assigned" a disproportionate amount of busy work) Prilly also found herself, in spite of herself, enjoying Janice's company. More than that, she enjoyed having a collaborator. It was in stark contrast to the rest of her life.

Weeknights were different— less focused, more numb. When Prilly got home she ritualistically changed into her at-home clothing, poured a glass of wine and ordered take-out to be delivered (or warmed up take-out leftovers). She didn't do any real grocery shopping during this time but she did stop at the corner grocer for wine, coffee and cream, when she needed them. Sometimes she also picked up a salt bagel and cream cheese for the morning although she inevitably felt guilty about eating it. She spent these nights curled up on her couch eating, drinking and watching TV. The entertainment tabloid shows and movies of the week that she usually relied on immediately brought Pete to mind, and she knew she wasn't equipped to think about him without tumbling down a dark hole. So instead she turned to the home shopping networks which provided comfort. Over a period of a few weeks she started to feel as if the "home shopping ladies" were all members of a community that she was a part of. She knew the hosts; she knew their styles and senses of humor; she knew when they were exaggerating or even lying (although she didn't care); and she knew that they were always there smiling and complementing their viewers. She could count on them. Although she was routinely tempted she only bought a couple of items (a new set of sheets for her bed that promised to be as soft as a favorite old T-shirt and a beige patent leather work bag that gave her a rush in her heart as she opened the box and tore away the bubble wrap; the sheets turned out to be thin and cheap-feeling but she kept them and tried to convince herself that they were better than they were; she loved the bag which she felt paid for itself when Janice remarked on it during one of their lunches at Nicos saying it was "very cool"). Mostly she just liked watching the programming. She felt it gave her somewhere to go at the end of the day, where she wasn't alone.

The weekends were much harder. She never left her apartment and found it hard to pass the time. She thought about organizing her closet, cleaning her apartment and even working; but she wasn't able to do any of this. She didn't even bother to shower or dress. It was as if all of the energy she was able to muster during the work week completely drained her on the weekend. She slept as late as possible, sometimes just lying in bed for hours to pass time. She frequently napped during the day and continued to watch home shopping. The worst part of the weekends was how much time she spent thinking about and missing Pete. It was actually all she could think about. She thought about how much better her weekends were when they were together and she felt truly alive.

It was on the sixth Saturday that Prilly decided to make a change. Unfortunately, it was a change for the worse. Falling back into dangerous territory she decided to make herself look as fabulous as possible, and casually walk by the teahouse Pete hung out at. She wasn't going to talk to him; she wasn't even going to go in; she just wanted a glimpse. She knew it was pathetic and a backward step but once she got the idea it took over, and she couldn't stop herself from doing it. Her heart was racing the whole cab ride, which she interpreted as being "alive" again. Before she knew it she was pulling up to the teahouse. Her nervous rush of energy immediately transformed into something else. She couldn't believe her eyes. She couldn't believe the timing. Pete was standing outside with Clyde. Just as the cab stopped Pete, looking hotter than ever, touched Clyde's face and leaned in to kiss her. Prilly was trembling. She started to hear buzzing in her ear and she thought she might pass out. "Drive! Drive!" she said. The driver had already stopped the car so he turned around and asked, "What? This isn't where you want to go?"

"Please just go. Take me back to my apartment. I'm so sorry but I forgot something. I need to go back," she said in a panic.

"You got it."

As they pulled away Prilly couldn't help but turn around and look through the rear windshield. Pete and Clyde were just standing there, and she couldn't be sure whether or not they had seen her. They drove over a pothole, and she gagged, choking back vomit.

All she could think about on the ride back was what a loser she was. She only hoped that he hadn't seen her. Even though she figured he must have known how pathetic she was, she didn't want to publicly confirm it, not again. After paying the outrageous taxi fare, as well as a huge tip because she was too embarrassed to ask for change, she entered her apartment and walked straight to the bathroom. She stared at her reflection in the bathroom mirror. She wanted to remember how ugly this particular shade of desperation was. She wanted to hate herself.

She spent the rest of the weekend in her normal routine of alternating between watching home shopping and sleeping. She didn't cry. She just tried to completely tune out.

Prilly picked herself up Monday for work. She and Janice were making a lot of progress on the memoir series. That Thursday night as Prilly was sitting on the couch and eating the last egg roll from her takeout, her phone rang. It was startling because her phone never rang. She was on a no-call list so she rarely even received telemarketing calls. She muted the TV and sat, listening. It was Pete. She listened to him leaving a message in his sexiest, hushed voice. "Hey there, you" and after a pause, "I've been thinking about you. I miss you. Give me a call. Bye."

Although there was an initial jolt of excitement that he had called, it immediately morphed into mortification as she assumed he had seen her that day in the cab. Why else would he be calling now, after all this time? She promised herself that she wouldn't call him, and, despite every urge to the contrary, she didn't. It was torture.

As the days and eventually weeks passed, Prilly, still fighting the craving to call him, did start to feel like she could expand the bounds of what was possible from just Chinese take-out and home shopping, to some grocery shopping, cooking and movie rentals. One Friday night standing in her local video store, she found herself perusing the foreign films looking at some of the movies Pete had told her she "positively must see" that he couldn't believe she had not seen. She rented a couple of them and bought a tub of microwave butter-flavored popcorn. That night, she made spaghetti with jarred marinara, opened a bottle of Cabernet and popped one of the movies in. It was a French film about an aspiring novelist and his tempestuous lover. It was beautiful, inspiring, romantic and devastating. It was just the kind of film she would have watched with Pete. Halfway through both the film and the wine she thought that the story was reminiscent of the life she had imagined living with him. And then, all of a sudden, the narrator interrupted her thoughts. He was describing how the male lead viewed his lover and he said, among other familiar things, that she possessed a "tinsel heart." In her wine-haze, Prilly nearly slid off the couch. She paused the movie and sat upright. Then she replayed the scene several times. "Tinsel heart. Tinsel heart. Tinsel heart." It suddenly occurred to her that it wasn't just that Clyde was beautiful and had been with Pete that hurt Prilly so deeply; it was the way he spoke of Clyde. He had a knack for making beauty where there was none, just as he made doubt. And he made what was already beautiful sound even more so, like Clyde. She had never been able to escape the "tinsel heart" remark until now. Until she realized that it wasn't his original thought. It was a line he lifted from a movie. Suddenly she couldn't stop wondering what other ideas he had espoused that weren't his own. Over the weekend she watched the other films and googled the many authors, artists and books he had urgently recommended. Soon she realized that most of his ideas were derivative of someone else's including his supposed insights about the artists they had seen, like Fairey and Modigliani. There was very little about art or philosophy that he had ever said to her that developed in his own mind. Even his ideas about love and relationships and being "in the moment" were rip-offs from one of his favorite authors, whom Prilly had never bothered to read before. Sunday night she watched the "tinsel heart" scene one more time and vowed never again. It was freeing. She felt stronger than she ever had before.

*

February was a very snowy month. The city was covered in white, then gray, then white again. The snow made Janice think of her childhood. By the end of February she would be sitting at her laptop at the end of her dining room table and suddenly see a childhood memory in between her and the screen. They were usually happy memories at these moments, like going sledding with her sister or making a pot of soup with her mother. But the memories always ended with either an awful image of her drunken father quieting their laughter or, more often, the memory of how badly she had always missed him in those happy moments. She wished he would have taken her sledding, even once. She shuddered at those thoughts and tried to avoid the distraction of nostalgia. This year the never-ending snow somehow made it difficult.

One brutally cold dark night in early March Kyle was making a cup of hot chocolate in the kitchen. Janice walked in to get some grapes to snack on, and he offered to make her a cup too. Usually she would say "no thanks," but on that blistery night she paused and then said, "Ok, that'd be nice. Thanks." She returned to the dining room, and a few minutes later Kyle walked in holding two white mugs filled with piping hot cocoa. "We didn't have any whipped cream or marshmallows or anything," he said as he handed her a mug.

"Oh that's all right, Honey. This smells good. I haven't had hot cocoa in as long as I can remember."

As he was walking out of the room Kyle asked, "Why don't you come in the living room with me and we can watch a movie or something?"

"Oh, well…" Janice started and, then, the smell of hot cocoa wafting between them, "Well ok. I guess I could wrap up early tonight." And with that the two of them walked into the living room each holding their mug. They sat on the couch and Kyle turned the TV on. He put on the TV Guide channel and they found a showing of the old film noir "Double Indemnity" that had just started a few minutes earlier. Kyle flipped to the station, and they sat silently and watched the movie while sipping their cocoa.

When the movie was over Janice ordered a large spinach and mushroom pizza with wheat crust. When it arrived Kyle took a couple of slices up to his room. He wanted to try and get in touch with Tash whom he had not seen since New Year's. They had texted a few times but he was growing worried. Most of his texts were unanswered including all of the ones asking her to get together. Janice stayed in the living room, watching the beginning of another old movie, "The Postman Always Rings Twice", as she ate a slice of pizza. When the movie was over she went back to her laptop. She closed out her work documents and got online. She went to Expedia and booked an open-ended round trip ticket to Detroit.

PART THREE

Kyle was cool and calm under almost any circumstance, but as he sat in the deli waiting for Tash he felt something unfamiliar: nerves. He'd barely spoken to her in two months, and he practically stalked her via text-messaging before pinning her down for brunch. After New Year's he knew she was in bad shape, but he didn't know how bad, and he was afraid to find out. He was on his third cup of coffee by the time Tash finally arrived.

"Hey, sorry I'm late. Did you order?" she asked robotically as she slid into the booth opposite him. "There's jelly on this seat, gross," she continued, making a face as she attempted to wipe it off with napkins she quickly pulled from the dirty dispenser on their table.

Kyle gave her a quick scan. She was wearing a long thin white sweater with black leggings, silver studded black boots and a black leather motorcycle jacket. She had several long silver strands around her neck and large silver hoop earrings. Her stick straight hair looked messier than usual and she was wearing her signature bright pink lipstick. She looked thin, too thin, and when she removed her large black sunglasses he noticed darkening under her eyes.

"So… what's been going on with you?" Kyle asked.

"I need coffee. Where's the waitress?" Tash asked while looking over her shoulder. "I need some fucking coffee like pronto."

Kyle put his hand up to signal to their nearby waitress. The white haired woman turned to them and asked, "What'll ya have?" while looking at her pad, pen in hand, ready to scribble down the order.

"She'll have a coffee too, and we'll share a large platter of blueberry cheese blintzes please," Kyle said while handing her both menus. "Thank you," he said as he looked back over to Tash who was still obsessed with the jelly on her seat.

"So, what's been going on with you?" Kyle asked again. "I guess you've been really busy lately."

"What's that?" Tash asked, finally looking up. "Oh, yeah, I have been really busy. Sorry to be so out of touch lately. I lost my phone for a week too; so I was out of touch with like everyone. It eventually turned up at Jacob's behind a couch cushion and with a totally dead battery. I didn't have a charger there either. What's going on with you?"

"Not much, same old same old," Kyle said as the waitress came over with Tash's coffee and a plate of bagel chips and spread. "Thank you," he said looking up.

Tash immediately poured sugar and creamer into her coffee. "It's about time you old fossil," she muttered as the waitress walked away.

Kyle grabbed a poppy-seed bagel chip and dipped it in the cream cheese spread. "I missed these, they're so good," he said as he took a bite. Tash was already half way done with her coffee and trying to signal the waitress for more. "Hey, have a bagel chip. I see some of those nasty cinnamon raisin ones you like," he said pointing at the plate.

"No, not in the mood," she replied. "I just desperately need some more coffee. It's so freaking cold too."

"Yeah, it's been like one big blizzard since we've seen each other," Kyle said. "So, what you been up to?"

"Oh, you know; same old. School, hanging with Jacob, doin' my thing. Lyric and I have been shopping in the village a lot lately, you know, the vintage clothes stores. It's super fun. We go on the hunt for something, like a Marilynesque stole or something, and we look around until we can dig one up. I'm going shabby-chique!" she said with laughter. "She's dating Jacob's roommate now. Did I tell you that? So we hang out there at the apartment all the time. Jeremy's kind of a jerk but whatever. He only likes to do her up the butt! Can you believe that? But she takes it because he buys her anything she wants and he's super hot. She's basically like his whore but whatever. Anyway, what about you? Anything new? How's Sam?"

Kyle could barely put his thoughts together after Tash's barrage. He couldn't understand why Lyric would be into a guy like that, and why Tash would think these guys were cool. He tried to focus on the last part of what she said-- and refocus the conversation. "Sam is going nuts. Remember that guy I told you his mom is seeing, the cruise guy?" Tash nodded and Kyle continued, "Well he's worried they're gonna get married."

"Does he hate the guy or something? Is he an asshole?" Tash asked before gulping down the last of her coffee.

"No, it's not like that. He's just some nice nerdy guy. He's been really nice to Sam's mom and he's pretty cool to Sam too. I don't know what Sam's deal is. I think it's more bullshit than anything."

"Uh huh," Tash said, though she was clearly distracted. She was motioning to her empty coffee cup as the waitress walked by. "Well, it doesn't sound so bad. Maybe he just doesn't want to be crowded, you know? To have another person to deal with," she continued as her eyes widened at the sight of the waitress approaching with a pot of coffee.

"Yeah, maybe," Kyle said. "I'm sure he'll get over it. He's close to his mom, he wants her to be happy." Then Kyle paused, watching Tash fix her second cup of coffee. "Listen, Tash, I've been kinda worried about you."

Tash's face didn't look as if she had registered the comment. Kyle took a breath in preparation for continuing when the waitress plopped down the platter of blintzes and two small plates in front of them.

"Those smell good," Kyle said, thankful for the respite. He grabbed a plate and spooned three blintzes onto it.

"Yeah, I'm not that hungry," Tash said.

"Oh no. You have to have the blintzes," Kyle replied, holding his fork up as if throwing down a battle call.

Tash giggled. "Well, if you put it that way, I'll nibble a little."

"That's better," Kyle said smiling. He then stabbed a blintz with his fork and put it on Tash's plate. They both started eating. After taking a few bites Kyle tried again, saying, "I've been a little worried about you. You've been hard to get a hold of and," at which point Tash interrupted him. "Yeah, yeah I know I've been busy and I told you about my phone."

"Yeah, it's not just that you've been tough to get in touch with. It's more than that. You've seemed different lately. Maybe it's since

Jacob; I don't know. I'm just worried about you. Do you really think this guy is good for you? He seems a little sketchy."

Kyle knew if he said too much Tash might completely withdraw so in an effort to keep it light he kept eating while talking, even putting a second blintz on Tash's plate although she hadn't finished the first one yet.

"Well, I mean, he's not the forever guy. That's for sure. But he's really into me, and I'm gonna ride the wave. I like having his place to veg in for a few days at a time. It's cool. Don't worry so much. I'm fine."

Knowing that when a woman said she was "fine" the conversation ends or enters dangerous territory, he let it go with, "Ok, I don't mean to pester you. Just checking-up."

"It's ok," she said, now smiling coyly as if to show she was the same old Tash he always knew. "I'm good, just partying a little, havin a thiiing you know. It's all good."

Kyle nodded.

"You're so sweet though. Little cousin always looking out for me. I promise I'll try to be better about checking in." With that she fetched a cinnamon raisin bagel chip and said, "I just can't resist."

Kyle smiled but the smile was a lie. Tash had all but confirmed what he was thinking: she wasn't doing well but she still had enough spunk to pretend that she was.

When Kyle got home that day he walked straight upstairs to his room where he took his cell phone out of his pocket before throwing his coat on the floor. He was about to sit on his bed when he noticed a folded piece of paper on his pillow. He opened it up. Three twenty dollar bills fell out and there was a note that read: "Kyle, have to go out of town for a couple days. Order yourself take-out, Dad will be home late. Fresh fruit in the fridge; don't let it go bad. I have my cell. Mom."

Kyle put the $60 on his dresser, kicked off his sneakers and lay back in bed leaning his pillows against the wall for support. He sent Sam a text: "Yo, wanna come over 2night and get pizza or something, my treat? Folks gone. Gotta vent. Finally saw Tash."

A few seconds later Sam replied: "Sure. I'll c u in 2 hrs."

Prilly had played Pete's message over and over and over again. She wanted to delete it but couldn't quite bring herself to, and she figured as long as no one else knew there was no harm in deriving the little pleasure she got from playing it. The pleasure she got from allowing herself to wonder, if only the littlest bit, if he really did miss her. She had promised herself that no matter what she wouldn't again humiliate herself by daring to call him back. So now she had a new routine. She would do her best to work while in the office (and try to keep up with Janice whom she continued to grow fond of despite the fact that every nicety or even bit of normalcy that Janice threw her way was always tempered with cutting comments and stacks of busy work), and when she got home at night she would change into her at-home clothes, open a bottle of wine, order take-out, listen to Pete's message and then make her way into the living room for a night of home shopping.

Then one particularly blah evening as she was cutting into her steaming egg roll the telephone rang. The noise was so startling that she flinched and then immediately hoped it was him. She wouldn't call him; but if somehow he called her again she wasn't sure what she would do. She got up and walked over to the answering machine to stand by it as her away message ended and the incoming message began. "Hey you," Pete said in his unmistakable voice before taking a deep throaty breath. He slowly continued; "Just wanted to see what you were up to girl. Came across something that made me think of you." He paused and then continued, "I miss you. Well…" and with that, she picked up the phone. "Hey."

"Oh," he said with his characteristic little laugh. "You're there."

"Yeah, I didn't hear the phone but then I heard you talking into the machine," Prilly nervously replied.

"Oh, I see," he said, again with his characteristic little laugh. "Well, I was just thinking about you and so I thought I'd be spontaneous and give you a call. I'm glad you picked up. It's good to hear your voice," he said in his sexiest.

Prilly's heart was racing. What was she doing? Why did she pick up the phone and how would she ever hang up. "Good to hear yours too," she said sheepishly.

"You want to hop in a cab and come over?" he asked.

"Um, I don't think that's such a good idea."

"But do you want to?" he pressed.

"I want to do what's good for me and…" but Pete cut her off, "Hey, we were good. We were really good, and I think you know it."

"Why are you calling now? So much time has passed and, and I never heard from you once after New Year's and you must have known how upset I was."

"That's not true, I did call you. I left you a message recently. Didn't you get it?"

"I'm not talking about that. I'm talking about New Year's. You didn't come after me, you didn't call, nothing. So why now?" Prilly felt stupid letting him know how she had expected him to chase after her, but she couldn't hold it in.

"Well, I miss you I guess. Just thought of you. Do I need a reason?"

"Are you seeing anyone?" Prilly asked with trepidation.

"Oh, not that again. There you go girl, I call to tell you I miss you, and you ask if I'm seeing anyone else."

Prilly didn't say a word, waiting for Pete to fill the void.

"Right now I want to see you," he finally said. Then there was a long silence again and Prilly said, "I assume you're seeing someone else by now. Are you?"

"Well hell, I'm just trying to follow my heart. I miss you. We had the beginning of something special. Didn't you know that? I know you did. No I haven't been sitting around all this time waiting for you, but, fuck, so what?"

"Look," Prilly said quietly, before taking a deep breath, "I can't do that again. I know you're seeing Clyde. I saw you with her and…"

but Pete cut her off. "Oh, geeze girl, here we go again. You've got to be kidding. Are you following me or something?"

"No, not at all," Prilly quickly chimed in, mortified and wishing she hadn't answered the phone. "I was just driving by and saw you two a while ago and…" and again Pete cut her off with, "Look, sure I've slept with Clyde a few times. She's beautiful, and it is what it is; but I've slept with lots of people. So what? We don't own each other. You're the one I miss. Keep your eyes on the big picture."

"I am, and that's why I can't do this. I just can't. Please don't call me again," Prilly said, trembling from nerves as she hung up the phone.

She stood there, balancing on the wall for a minute waiting to see if he would call back. He didn't. She returned to the living room couch, refilled her wine glass and started to drink. About fifteen minutes later she started to eat her lukewarm Chinese food. More than anything she wished she could have jumped in a cab and that she would be with Pete just for a night, but she couldn't bear the humiliation anymore. It was enough that she was privately humiliated; she couldn't let him or anyone else see it. And she could never look at him without seeing him making love with Clyde, looking into her eyes, beautiful Clyde, not before he knew her, but after. That image was a shameful reminder of everything Prilly feared she never was and never would be, which she felt he had just confirmed. She wanted to keep it secret. Two days later she deleted the only message she had saved. She continued with her daily routine of work, takeout and television.

Janice only had a few minutes at the gate before she had to board her flight. While standing in the pre-boarding line she called her mother from her cell phone.

"Hello," Myra answered.

"Hi, Mom, it's me."

"Jannie?" Myra asked quizzically.

"Yes, Mom."

"Oh, hi dear. I'm surprised to hear from you in the middle of the week," Myra said, sounding both happy and surprised.

"Well I'm actually calling from the airport Mom. I'm on my way to see you. I wanted to visit Dad."

"The airport? You're at the airport, oh my. Let me call Margie and see if she can pick you up. I know Scott must be working with his big job and all, but maybe Margie can come and get you. Or maybe..."

As Myra started to trail off Janice interrupted with, "No, Mom. I'm at La Guardia Airport in New York. I have to go in a minute, they just started boarding my flight."

"Oh, well when do you get in? I'm sure I can have Margie or..." Janice cut her off, "Mom, Mom, it's ok. I've already reserved a rental car."

"Oh, ok Honey. Well how long are you staying for? Are Richard and Kyle coming with you? I so would love to meet that grandson of mine. The pictures you sent are all on the fridge." Janice tried to interrupt but it was impossible as Myra continued: "Shall I set up your room for you? I have some of your father's things stored in there but..."

Finally Janice jumped in saying, "No, no, it's all right Mom. I've booked a room at the Westin down the road from you. It's only me and I can only stay for a day or two."

"All right dear. Well come over for dinner tonight after you freshen up at your hotel. I'll make something special. Your dad will be so happy to see you. He's been feeling…"

"Mom, I have to go. I have to board my flight."

"Ok dear; have a good trip. I'll call Marge and see if she and the kids can come…" Myra was going to continue when Janice said more forcefully, "I have to go Mom, I'll see you in a few hours."

"Bye Jannie."

"Bye Mom."

*

Janice brought her work bag overflowing with manuscripts, book proposals and her notes about the memoir series. She intended to keep as busy as possible. She worked the entire flight sipping on a club soda and snacking on some whole wheat pretzels. Twenty minutes before landing, a flight attendant announced that all tray tables must be placed back in their upright and locked position and personal items must be stored. Janice quickly put her work away and sat staring out of the window for the remainder of the flight. It was the first time she stopped to think about what she was doing. Suddenly she felt afraid-- afraid of the state she would find her father in and afraid to face her mother since she hadn't been back to visit in all this time, even after her father's accident. She was also afraid to see Marge. Even though they were close, Marge had been stuck with the lion's share of dealing with their parents, and Janice knew it. Since the accident Marge had begun to mention this in ways she never had before. She thought about all of these things, and she thought about how she had vowed never to go back. Despite all of these thoughts as the plane taxied down the runway she leaned her head against the window, looking out, feeling glad to be there.

After a long wait at the car rental kiosk, and a longer drive in rush-hour traffic, she arrived at her hotel. She checked in, unpacked her small suitcase and transferred her wallet and keys from her work bag into her Prada handbag. Then she washed her hands, brushed her teeth and hair, put on some fresh deodorant and headed out. A few minutes later she was pulling into the driveway of her family home.

When she turned off the ignition she paused for a minute, looking at the tiny yellow house. The paint was chipping badly. Then she threw her keys into her bag, walked to the front door, held the screen door open and pressed the rusty old doorbell.

Suddenly the front door swung open. "Oh, Jannie, I'm so happy to see you! Let me look at you. Let me look at you!" her mother exclaimed. Her mother was standing in a white housedress with blue polka dots shouting "let me look at you" over and over again while grinning ear to ear.

"Hi Mom," Janice said softly, noticing how impossibly old her mother now looked.

"Well come in Honey, come in."

As Janice stepped into the doorway she felt as if she were entering a lost world in slow motion. It was as if the house had shrunk; it was a miniature version precisely preserved as if from her memory, a memory she didn't even know she had. As her mother closed the door behind her she just stood, looking around and feeling as if she had walked into a haunted doll house. It was so much smaller than she had remembered. She looked to the left into the cramped living room. Nothing had changed-- the couch, her father's old recliner looking even older, the buttercup walls were dirty as ever as were the see-through white drapes. The only difference was that their old little TV and stand had been replaced with a slightly larger version of each.

"Well, let me look at you," Myra said again, staring at Janice who was staring into the living room.

"Oh, sorry Mom, it's been so long since I've been here, it just…" and then Janice couldn't find the words so Myra said, "It must have taken you back a minute."

"Yes, well, I'm fine," Janice said, trying to regroup.

Myra flung her arms open, "Well, give me a hug Honey."

Janice leaned in and hugged her. As she was going to pull away Myra held on and hugged her tighter. It was a long, strong, complete hug. Janice couldn't remember the last time anyone had hugged her like that; so she gave into it, for a moment.

"Well, give me your coat and then come in the kitchen Honey and see your father."

Janice took off her coat and followed Myra into the kitchen. It too was exactly as she remembered, only much smaller. The rectangular Formica table sat in the middle of the light blue kitchen, with a small bouquet of multi-colored flowers placed in the center. Janice's father was sitting at the far end of the table. "Hi there Jan," he said, looking up at her.

"Hi Pop," she said, while giving him the once the over. "How are you?" she continued as she walked over and bent down to hug him, noticing the bodily waste bag connected to him, just slightly visible from under his dark blue robe. As he started to put his arms around her she pulled back and turned to her mother who was standing over the sink, looking out of the tiny window in front of her while drying her hands with a dishrag.

"Something smells good, what is that Mom?" Janice asked.

"Oh, would you look at that Mrs. Jensen. She's so nosey. Any unfamiliar car in the driveway and she finds an excuse to walk out onto her porch and look over. Even when it's freezing!"

"Mom, something smells good," Janice repeated.

"Oh, it's just meatloaf dear. I wanted to make something more special but with Margie and the kids not coming until tomorrow I thought..." at which point Janice cut her off, "Oh, Marge isn't coming?"

"Oh, she wanted too; she felt awful. It's just that Greg has some band practice he can't get out of. He has a recital coming up you know. I invited her over tomorrow night. I'm making pot roast, your favorite," she said gleefully.

"Oh, well I wasn't sure if I was going to go home tomorrow or the next day," Janice said as she glanced to her left and noticed all of Kyle's wallet-size school photos on their old olive green refrigerator, along with some crayon drawings Marge's kids must have made.

"Well I figured you would stay for at least two nights. We haven't seen you in so long Jannie. You can stay can't you?" Myra asked, now turning directly to her.

"Sure," Janice said, as she took a seat at the table, leaning back to hang her handbag on the corner of her chair as if she were a guest in a stranger's house. Myra noticed and said, "Let me take that for you and put it in the living room."

"That's all right Mom, I'm fine," Janice replied. Next to the little vase there was a large bowl of green grapes just as there had always been. Janice picked a few and after popping one into her mouth she said, "You know Mom, grapes keep much better if you store them in the fridge."

"I put them in the fridge every night and just take them out during the day. If I left them in there I'm worried we'd forget to eat them," Myra said as she walked over to the oven and removed a large meatloaf surrounded by roasted carrots. The room suddenly got warm and was filled with smells that Janice was no longer used to. Myra put a slice of meatloaf on each of the three plates stacked beside her, along with one carrot, and a scoop of mashed potatoes out of a stained pot on the stove. She served Janice first. "Oh, thank you Mom. This looks delicious."

After serving everyone Myra got a pitcher of ice tea from the refrigerator and a basket of crescent rolls from the counter and finally sat down opposite her husband.

"Well, we're so glad you're here Jannie, aren't we?" Myra said, looking over to her husband.

"We sure are," Janice's father said, as he mustered up a half smile.

"It's a blessing; a real blessing. Well, let's start eating," Myra said. "Jannie, can I pour you some ice tea?" Myra asked, lifting the pitcher.

"Yes, thank you," Janice said raising her glass. "This really smells good. I haven't had meatloaf in as long as I can remember," she continued. "You still do the tomato sauce strip on top the same way," she said as she took her first bite.

"Why mess with a classic, I always say," her mother replied.

"It's very good Ma," Janice said as she continued to eat.

After a few minutes of eating in silence Myra said, "So, tell us about the big city. How are Richard and Kyle?"

"They are fine. Kyle is doing very well in school. He is a hard worker and he's very gifted. Richard is doing extremely well at work. He's very busy; we both are. Everything is fine," she said before taking another bite of buttery potatoes.

"Tell us about your work Jannie. It sounds so exciting making books," Myra said, smiling at Janice.

"Well I don't exactly make the books but…"

"Oh," Myra said, embarrassed, "I meant…"

"No, it's ok Ma, I know what you mean. It is exciting. It's very exciting actually. I have been given a lot of new responsibilities. It's very demanding but it's worth it. I am publishing a new line of memoirs. The press has never done anything like this and the whole project was my idea, my work, everything. It's going to be a very big hit. The series is scheduled to premier in less than two months so I've really been under a lot of pressure."

"Oh, well, that sounds very impressive. My, isn't that impressive?" Myra said, beaming and looking from Janice to her husband.

"Yes, it sure is," Janice's father said.

They continued to eat and then a few minutes later Myra asked, "So, I was surprised to get your phone call. We were so happy you were coming to visit. What made you decide to come so last minute?"

"Oh, well I hope I didn't put you out," Janice started before Myra jumped in, "No, no dear, not at all. We are very happy you came, very happy. I was just taken aback."

"Well, I've been working so hard on my memoir series and… and there is a potential author in Detroit who I've been having trouble signing so I thought I would come and meet with him in person."

"Oh, I see," Myra said, sounding a bit deflated.

"So it was a chance to see you and Dad which I've been meaning to do," Janice said, regretting the lie and making it sound like visiting them was just another item on her "to do" list. But she couldn't backtrack.

"Well we're just glad you had time to come and see us. So you'll take care of your business tomorrow and then come over for a big family dinner. We can celebrate all of your wonderful accomplishments," Myra said.

"That sounds great Ma," Janice said, feeling uncomfortable.

When they finished eating Myra cleared the dishes and put up a pot of decaffeinated coffee. "I made a pound cake."

"Thanks Mom but I'm stuffed and I'm really tired, I think I should get back to my hotel," Janice said.

"Oh, won't you have just a little slice Honey? I made that lemon icing you like," Myra said, turning to Janice and holding a plate with a small iced loaf on it.

Janice felt terribly bloated already but said, "Sure, I'll stay for a sliver. It looks great Mom."

"Some decaf?" Myra asked, holding out the pot.

"Sure. Thank you."

Fifteen minutes later Janice got up and walked over to her father. She leaned in and gave him a little hug. "Night Pop, see you tomorrow."

She grabbed her bag and walked over to the door, followed by her mother.

"Are you sure you don't want to bring a snack back to the hotel? I can fix you something real quick?" Myra asked.

"Thanks but that's ok Mom. Thank you for dinner. Everything was delicious."

"Oh, we're just so happy to see you Honey. We're so happy you came. Your father has been saying so since you called. It's the first time he's eaten at the kitchen table since, since you know. I usually have to bring his meals into the bedroom."

Janice smiled. "I'll see you tomorrow night. Around 6:00, ok?" Janice asked as she leaned in and gave her mother a hug.

"We'll see you at 6:00. Come earlier if your work is finished. We'll be here, come any time," Myra hollered as Janice walked to her car.

*

After an early morning workout in the hotel gym followed by a day of work in her hotel room, Janice arrived at her parents' house at exactly 6:00 o'clock. She rang the doorbell, and her sister Marge immediately opened the door. "Hey, Jan! Great to see you! Come on in."

Marge leaned in to hug Janice as she entered the house, but before they really connected Greg, Marge's 10 year old ran into the room whizzing a little airplane in his hand as if he were flying it, quickly followed by his younger brother Tim who was chasing him. Distracted, Marge turned and yelled, "I told you two to stop running, this instant."

"Come in, take your coat off Jan," Marge said, returning her attention to Janice who was standing just inside the doorway. "It's so good to see you. I can't believe you're here."

Janice walked in, shutting the door behind her. She took off her coat and hung it on the coat rack along with her handbag. "Something smells good," Janice said.

"Mom's going crazy in there, roast beef, all the fixings; gravy, peas, stuffing; she probably hasn't stopped cooking all day," Marge said as she plopped down onto the couch.

"She didn't have to go to all that trouble," Janice said.

"Don't be silly; you know Mom lives for this sort of thing," Marge replied at which point Myra came into the living room carrying two glasses of ice tea. She placed them down on the coffee table and gave Janice a big hug. "Hi Honey, I'm just finishing up in the kitchen; so why don't you and your sister catch up. I bought that fancy port wine cheddar cheese spread you used to like. It's right there with some Ritz crackers," Myra said, pointing to a small plate on the coffee table.

"Thanks Mom; that looks great," Janice said. "Can I help you with dinner?"

"Oh no dear, just sit and catch up with Marge and dinner will be ready soon," Myra said as she walked back into the kitchen.

Janice sat down beside her sister on the small couch. "So, the kids have grown so much. They look great. You look great," she nervously said picking up her ice tea.

"You look great too. So skinny. You must be on one of those New York celebrity diets right? What is it the zone, the ozone, the…" and with that Marge laughed before finishing the sentence.

"Well, I just try to eat healthy," Janice said slightly defensively.

"Relax, I'm jealous," Marge quipped back.

"Where's Scott?" Janice asked.

"He felt terrible but he couldn't make it. He put in a bid for a big job downtown and got the contract. They broke ground a few days ago and he's been working late ever since. Honestly…" Marge said leaning in and lowering her voice, "As much as he wanted to see you, I think he's had enough of Mom and Dad. He's been here a lot helping out over the past few months, and I think he needs a break, and this new job is just the excuse." Janice understood.

Marge then turned her attention to the cheese plate in front of them. "You know you're the only one that has ever gotten Mom to buy this cheese. And I love this cheese!" she proclaimed as she made a little cheese sandwich in between two crackers.

Janice smiled awkwardly and leaned in to take a cracker with some cheese spread, which she thought looked vile. "Well it sounds like Scott is doing really well. That's great. I hope he gets paid for working late," Janice said as she bit into her cracker, the taste of neighborhood Christmas parties coming back as the cheese oozed in between her teeth.

"So, Jan," Marge said, leaning in and lowering her voice again, "What the hell brings you here?"

"Oh, well…," and as Janice tried to muster up an answer Marge's kids came in the room complaining that they were hungry. "Well take a couple of crackers," Marge said, "but don't get crumbs everywhere, grandma won't like that."

As the kids walked into the kitchen with their crackers Marge turned intently back to Janice, "Sorry, what were you saying?"

"Oh, well…"

"Mom said something about an author you had to meet with?" Marge inquired. "She even told me I couldn't call you today and bother you while you were working."

"Yes, that's right. I'm editing a new line of books, a big line actually, and I needed to meet with a potential author in Detroit; so I thought I could stop by and see everyone," Janice said, before eating the rest of her cracker.

"Jan, come on, it's me," Marge whispered. "Give it up. What's going on? You haven't come in all this time and now…" but they were again interrupted, this time by Myra who came in and proclaimed, "Dinner is ready. The boys are hungry; I think you two should come in."

Marge shot Janice a look like, "I'll get you later," as they both stood up and walked into the kitchen holding their ice tea glasses. The table was overcrowded with platters of food. It looked like Thanksgiving or Christmas. The boys were already sitting on one side of the table. Myra told Marge to sit opposite her boys and that Janice should take the end seat. "But where's Dad going to sit," Janice asked?

"Oh, dear, your father isn't feeling well. It's a bad day today. He just can't make it to the table so I fixed him a tray. He feels terrible with you here and all but you can go and say hi after dinner," Myra explained as she sat down, setting down a bowl of peas which completed the feast. "Well, let's eat everyone," she said.

*

After dinner Myra started clearing the dishes. The boys asked if they could go and play, to which Marge said, "Just be good; don't make a mess." She then asked, "Mom, can I help you with the dishes?" Janice followed her lead with, "Oh, can I help you Mom?"

"No, no, girls. I'm just going to get a pot of coffee on over here and you girls can bring dessert to your father. I know he really wanted to visit with you Jannie," she said turning away from the dishes towards Janice.

"Oh, you don't need to go to the trouble Mom. I'm stuffed," Janice said.

"Oh, it's no trouble. I made one of your favorites, apple cobbler. I would have made peach but you know they aren't in season yet. You can just have a little dear. Besides, I know your father really wants to see you. He can't resist my cobbler, even at his crankiest." And with that Myra took the Saran wrap off of the big casserole dish that had been sitting on the counter. As she peeled away the plastic wrap swirls of cinnamon filled the room. Janice suddenly remembered long days of playing outside with Marge in their secret fortress and then returning to the house, dripping with dirt, to the smell of freshly baked cobbler just out of the oven. Before she knew it, Myra was handing Janice a dessert bowl with cobbler and a scoop of vanilla ice cream melting on top. "That's for your father dear; you and Margie can bring it to him and have a little visit, and by then the decaf will be brewed and you can come in for dessert. I made ginger snap cookies for the boys, and I thought you might want to bring a few home Jannie, for Kyle. Oh Margie, there's plenty for Scott too. I'll make him a care package so he can have a nice hot dinner when he gets home."

"Thanks Mom," Marge said.

Janice remained sitting at the table, holding her father's dessert. "Oh, well here you go dear," Myra said, handing her a napkin and spoon. "Everything will be ready in about ten minutes."

Janice stood up and she and Marge walked to her parents' bedroom. The door was closed so Marge knocked. They heard grumbling on the other side saying something like "come in."

As Janice followed Marge into the small room that had seemed so much bigger as a child, she looked at the old embattled man lying in his bed who also seemed so much bigger when she was a child. There were two small dimly lit lamps on each nightstand, providing the only light in the bleak room. Janice's father was sitting up in bed, propped up against several pillows. Marge sat in the only chair in the room, in a corner near a small window. Janice handed her father his dessert, looked over at Marge and then sat on the edge of the bed.

"Thank you," he mumbled. "But I'm not hungry."

As Janice outstretched her hand to the take bowl back Marge piped in with, "Just eat the cobbler Dad. Mom made it special. Just try it."

He nodded.

"So Dad, how are you feeling?" Marge asked, sounding annoyed. Janice thought about how Marge always sounded annoyed on the phone when talking about her father-- and apparently even when talking to him. Things hadn't improved between them despite his ailments. It was as if she couldn't hide her resentment that he was still in her life.

"I'm ok," he said, fidgeting around trying to get comfortable to eat. "How are the boys? How is Scott's new job going?" he asked before taking a bite of his cobbler.

"Everyone's fine Dad," Marge replied. "So, what about Janice Dad? She came all this way." It seemed as if Marge wanted to say more, with the meaning of her words revealed only by the tone.

"Yes. I'm just so glad you came Jan," he said, looking at Janice and trying to smile.

"I'm sorry you aren't feeling well Pop," Janice said. He took another bite of the cobbler and said, "This is really good. Aren't you two having any?"

"We'll join Mom in a bit. We wanted to see you first," Janice replied. "It smells good. I haven't had cobbler since I was living here," she said, smiling at her father.

"Yeah, well I can see why you wouldn't want the tastes of home," Marge said sarcastically.

"I remember how much you and I liked Mom's peach cobbler in the summer, do you remember that Dad?" Janice asked, trying to focus only on her father.

"He doesn't remember anything," Marge said.

Janice's father smiled half heartedly again at Janice and looked over at Marge, as if to plead for sympathy.

"You know what I remember," he said before pausing.

"What Pop, what do you remember?" Janice asked softly.

"That summer we went to the big fair in Ann Arbor. Do you remember that? This cobbler smells a lot like something they had there. Do you remember?"

"I think it was those apple donuts," Janice said. "Do you remember those donuts Marge?" she asked turning to her sister. We bought a bag and ate them the whole drive home."

Marge shook her head.

"Yes, that's what it was. The donuts," their father said, with another small smile.

"That was such a fun day. One of the best I remember," Janice said looking at him.

"You must not remember it then? Don't you remember all the beer Dad drank and him fighting with Mom about driving home? On the walk to the car he jumped and slammed his hand into that big sign, that big green metal freeway sign. Don't you remember? There was blood everywhere, and he was screaming," Marge said angrily.

Nobody responded, and after a couple of moments passed Janice said, "I remember having fun that day. It was the prettiest place I had ever seen. We had all of those tickets, those tickets for the rides and there was that rollercoaster and I had never been on anything like that before. And I remember you got us lots of treats that day," Janice said.

"Yes, that's right. I think you had cotton candy, and Marge, Marge you had an ice-cream cone right?" their father asked.

"I had a waffle ice cream sandwich," Marge said.

"That's right. Chocolate," he said.

"No Dad, it was strawberry," Marge said as she stood up and walked out of the room, forcefully shutting the door behind her.

Janice looked lovingly at her father. "Your cotton candy, it was pink right, bright pink?"

"Yes, Pop."

"Jannie, I don't blame you for not visiting. I know that…" but Janice cut him off. "I've been so busy, really, you can't imagine what it's like in New York. I just couldn't get away…"

"Jannie, it's ok. I understand."

"Pop, when you had your accident I wanted to…" but he again cut her off, this time taking her hand and looking intently at her: "Jannie, it wasn't an accident. It wasn't an accident."

Janice sat perfectly still, with her hand resting limply in his. "What do you mean Pop? Were you…" but she couldn't find the words so he helped her. "No. I wasn't drinking Jannie. I know you have no reason to believe this but I've been sober for a few years now. Your mother finally threatened to leave me, and she meant it. She packed a bag and went and stayed with one of those ladies from the Church. And, well, I couldn't do it without her. It was a battle but I've been sober." He paused again and finished, "I wasn't drinking that day."

He looked down and Janice moved her hand to really embrace his. "Well, what do you mean Pop, that it wasn't an accident?"

"It's been real hard Jannie, real hard. I don't remember much but I know what I am, and I know what I done to all of you. Your mother's been telling me for years how awful I was. When I think now," he shuddered and continued, "She was a young beautiful woman when I met her, and now she's almost done, she's almost done, and she's been stuck with me and my problem."

Janice could hardly believe what she was hearing. "What do you mean it wasn't an accident Pop?" she asked again.

"I know what I am, and I couldn't take it no more. I thought I would release your mother, release all of you. That maybe you'd visit her, and your sister wouldn't be so angry anymore. Wastin' her life with that damn anger, like a cancer. I just didn't see what was left at this end. That's why Jannie. That's why I did it. That's why I walked across that way like that. That's why. And now look at me. Look at your mother. I couldn't even do this right." He took a long pause and continued. "I never told your mother. She never asked."

Janice sat still and quiet with tears now rolling down her face. They didn't say anything else. A few minutes later she gave him a long hug and went to join Marge and her mother in the kitchen where she sat in silence eating cobbler and drinking decaf while they spoke about some shopping trip they were planning for the weekend.

When Janice left the house, she hugged her mother as completely as her mother had hugged her. Although she didn't say a word, Myra felt grateful.

When Janice arrived back in her house the next afternoon Kyle was sitting in the living room watching TV. She walked over to him, pulled a Ziploc bag of ginger snap cookies out of her bag and handed them to him. "I'm tired, I'm going to shower and maybe take a rest," she said.

"Ok, Mom. Thanks for the cookies," Kyle said, confused. He was preoccupied. He had a terrible feeling that something bad was going to happen, and he wished that Tash would respond to his many text messages.

Jeremy Bransfield spent most days sleeping late, playing video games, smoking pot with his roommate Jacob and sleeping with his girlfriend Lyric or whatever girl he could get up into his apartment. Although ragged and unkempt he was naturally good-looking, tall with great bone structure and intense dark eyes. He looked even better when compared to his roommate. Women often looked at Jacob as the grimy little pot guy and Jeremy as his hot roommate. But for all of his foolishness, Jacob was at the core a decent person who meant no harm. Jeremy, on the other hand, was smart, slick and far more dangerous than Jacob was capable of realizing.

Jacob met Jeremy when he came into the used record store looking for an obscure reggae artist. Soon Jeremy offered Jacob a "business opportunity" to deal dope out of the backroom of the store. With declining sales Jacob had been worried about losing his job. He also liked the idea of access to free pot; so he quickly agreed. A bumpkin in many ways, Jacob didn't realize that had been Jeremy's only real purpose for coming into that store on that day; so Jacob later gave Jeremy a reggae CD as a gift. Thinking he was quite clever, Jacob eventually started putting some of his cut of the drug profits into the cash register at the store, to stop the store from going under. Despite his profits from the illicit sales, he wanted to keep his job. It also made him feel like a good guy; a clever guy. Jeremy wanted to keep the location. The two became fast friends. Soon pot transformed into a full-fledged pharmacy of pills and powders that Jacob chose not to think too much about. And soon after the two became roommates. Jeremy thought this would make Jacob easier to monitor.

Every Tuesday Jeremy set his alarm clock for 7:00 am. He showered and was out of the apartment by 8:00, listening to headphones and carrying an old gray backpack. He spent the day traveling by trains and buses. First, he stopped and picked up bialys and cream cheese from a local bakery that boasted the best bialys in Brooklyn. Then he visited his grandmother in a nursing home in Queens. When he arrived she was sitting in her room at the little doily covered table next to the window. She always wore a dress on Tuesdays and was always waiting for his arrival. She asked a staff member to bring them some tea, and Jeremy fixed a bialy and cream cheese for each of them. Then they played cards or checkers. He stayed for exactly one hour, an hour that his grandmother looked forward to all week. He was her only visitor.

Three times a month this visit was followed by a series of errands or other meaningless activities. But on the fourth Tuesday of every month he made his way to a tenement in the South Bronx. There, he emptied his backpack filled with money and then refilled it with pills and powders. It was a long trip for a fast procedure. On his way back to the subway he stopped at a small Puerto Rican take-out restaurant. He bought a large garlic chicken plate, a large rice and beans and a large container of coconut drink. With his backpack on his shoulders, and carrying the take-out food, he made the long trip back to Brooklyn where he and Jacob chowed down. Melville smelled the garlic from his room. The next morning Jacob took the backpack to the store, unpacked and opened for business. This went on swimmingly until one cold Wednesday morning in March.

Tash had spent the night at Jacob's apartment. Although it seemed like she lived there, she normally went back to her dorm Mondays and didn't return until Thursday night so that she could attend her classes which met on Tuesdays and Thursdays. This week however was Spring break, and Tash wanted to spend it stoned at Jacob's. She wanted Lyric to stay too but Lyric was growing tired of the endless cycle of getting high and coming down. She began to feel that the apartment was like a vortex that slowly sucked time before anyone could notice. At this point, Lyric was just about done with "up-the-ass Jeremy", as she had come to think of him, and used Spring break as an excuse to get out of town with some of her friends. She was ready to sport a string bikini, guzzle some margaritas, and go down on a jock like the good old days. She wanted Tash to join her but Tash was living in another world. Tash was able to pull it together most weeks to go through the motions of going to her classes, but she was more of a squatter than a college student at this point. And so, this was the first Wednesday morning that Tash found herself in Jacob's apartment. Jacob got up and ready for work as usual, trying not to wake her. But as he was zipping up Jeremy's backpack Tash rolled over and sleepily said, "Hey. What's going on?"

"I gotta go to work, you know that Babe. Go back to sleep; you can just crash here today, and we'll hang when I get back."

Tash was groggy but she rubbed her eyes and tried to focus on what was happening. It suddenly occurred to her that with Jacob going to work she would be stuck in the apartment all day with Jeremy. "Wait, wait for me. I'll come with you," she said, sitting up and stretching her arms upward.

"Babe, that's sweet but I gotta go and you'll take forever. And you'll be bored anyway," Jacob retorted, while putting his jacket on.

Tash leapt from the bed revealing a hot pink tank top and white cotton underwear. "I'll be ready super fast. I can hang with you in the store, and if it gets boring I can bum around the village. Besides, I need to stop by my dorm at some point to pick up a few things. Just hold up for a couple minutes."

Jacob didn't think Jeremy would be happy if Tash tagged along that day; he was pissed the night before when he had to share the take-out with her, but looking at her, at how sexy she was, he found it hard to say no and figured it wasn't a big deal. "You gotta hurry, I can't be late."

"No problem. Give me five minutes," she said as pulled her jeans on.

Thirty minutes later they were on the train with two coffees they had picked up from a street vendor. Despite rush hour they managed to get two seats when some yuppies got off. Tash leaned on Jacob's shoulder the whole ride. Sometimes she would start to drift asleep but a bump or announcement from the conductor would jar her. Just before they arrived at their stop Tash, who was nodding off again, lost her grip on her coffee cup and spilled it in

Jacob's lap. He jumped up screaming "oh shit" which caused Tash to jump up and try to help. She found an old tissue in her pocket and manically started to wipe his pants as they arrived at their stop, bumping into people in the crowd as the train screeched into the station. She grabbed Jacob's coffee cup as they hurriedly tried to make their way off the bustling train. In all of the commotion Jacob left the backpack on his seat. He realized what he had done as soon as he was standing on the platform watching the train go by. It happened so quickly he could only stand there, with his heart racing.

"Holy shit, holy shit," he screamed, as he threw his arms up in the air and then rested his hands on his head in disbelief. Totally out of it, Tash asked, "What's wrong? Why are you freaking out?"

"The bag, the bag," he said, breathing heavily.

"You left your bag on the train?" Tash asked, rolling her eyes as if this was somehow an inconvenience for her. "Well, let's go find someone who works here and ask what you can do. They can probably call the driver or something or maybe there's a lost and found or something."

Jacob just stood, staring down the dark tunnel that lay before him. It was crowded and loud but he felt as though he stood alone. Everything was happening in slow motion. He could barely make out the words Tash was saying.

"Jacob, don't worry about it, I'm sure we'll get the bag back," Tash said, tapping his back. "Chill out."

"I'm dead. I'm so dead," he muttered.

"Come on, let's get out of here," Tash said.

"I gotta get to the store and call Jeremy."

"Why? Don't you think you should talk to someone here?" she asked. "Maybe they can get your bag."

"Come on, I gotta go and call Jeremy."

"Well, you can use my cell," she said, as she started to look around in her pocketbook.

"No, I'll call from the store. Let's get out of here. I'll explain it on the way."

*

Jacob sat solemnly in the backroom of the store, with the door closed. He was trembling when he picked up the phone to call Jeremy.

"Dude, it's me; something happened," he said as soon as Jeremy answered.

"What happened?" Jeremy asked.

"I left the backpack on the train. It's gone; the bag is gone."

"What the fuck? You left the fucking bag on the train?" Jeremy shouted. "How could you do something so stupid?" he continued.

"It was an accident. Tash spilled coffee on me and I was distracted and it just happened," Jacob said desperately.

"Tash, what the fuck was she doing there? Does she know what's in the bag?" Jeremy furiously demanded.

"No, no. She was just coming to hang out with me. She doesn't know anything," Jacob said, but Jeremy suspected he was lying. "She told me to call the train station and see if they found the bag. Do you think I should do that? Maybe we can get it back," Jacob said.

"Yeah, that sounds great, call and ask for the backpack filled with drugs. Have you lost your fucking mind?" Jeremy bellowed.

"Well I just thought maybe they wouldn't have opened it," Jacob said. "You know, like a privacy thing."

"Are you fucking kidding me? You gonna take that chance? Ten to one someone reported a backpack on the train, and the God damn bomb squad is down there."

"What do we do man?" Jacob pleaded.

"Let me think. Just let me think for a minute," Jeremy quipped back. After a long pause where the only sound Jacob heard was his own belabored breathing, Jeremy said, "Look, we have a few weeks. We have a few weeks to figure it out. Let's not do anything. Just work at the store today, and we can figure it later."

"Ok, ok," Jacob agreed, still trembling.

"And don't fucking bring that chick back with you, got it?" Jeremy said sternly.

"Yeah, ok," Jacob said before they each hung up.

*

Jacob persuaded Tash to spend the night at her place, but it wasn't easy, and she was pissed. He spent the day running different scenarios in his head of how this would all play out. He was able to convince himself that it would be all right. Everyone was entitled to a "free-be", and this was theirs. It would be ok. That night when he got back to his apartment Jeremy wasn't there. He waited in the living room for hours. Then, finally ready to go to bed, as he walked past Jeremy's bedroom, he had a frightening flash. He opened the door, and to his horror, the room was empty. It had been entirely cleared out. He opened the closet, and every drawer, but there was no sign of Jeremy; no sign that he had ever been there. He just stood there wondering what he had done, what he had gotten himself into and what he should do now.

Jacob spent the next three days getting stoned in his apartment. At one point he bumped into Melville in the kitchen. Melville asked why he wasn't at work and Jacob told him, "It's none of your fucking business." Tash was texting and calling incessantly but he didn't respond to her either. He kept thinking that he had a month to figure it out. He just needed to stay put and think. Then he received a phone call on the landline. It went straight to the machine and he heard Jeremy's voice say, "Pick up the phone."

He flew off of the couch and stumbled to the phone. "Hello, hello. Dude, Jeremy is that you?"

"Listen, you gotta get out of there."

"What do you mean? Where are you dude? Why'd you take off?" Jacob pleaded.

"Listen, you gotta get out of there."

"But we have four weeks, we have four weeks to figure this out," Jacob said.

"They watch the store. They know you haven't been there. They know there was no delivery. I don't know when they'll come looking, but it'll be soon. You gotta get out of there."

"But, but we can explain. Can't we explain what happened and ask for a break or something? We can like pay it back or something right?" Jacob asked frantically.

"You gotta get out of there," Jeremy said one last time before hanging up.

Jacob was motionless, holding the dead phone line, with ringing in his ears. He could feel his blood coursing through his body but his mind felt like it was stuck. He was completely frozen. He hung up the phone, walked over to the couch and searched for his cell. He sent Tash a text message:

"Need 2 c u pronto. On my way."

He didn't wait for a reply before he grabbed a duffle bag and threw some random clothes and CDs in. He took an envelope of cash he had stashed under his mattress and left.

*

When Jacob arrived at Tash's dorm, he was in such a full-fledged panic that he could barely stop shaking. It is for this and this reason alone that when Tash opened the door and saw him standing there she let him in. She had planned to leave him out in her hallway begging to come in, only to be rejected. She had spent the last few days livid at him. She was in such a bad way that she had not showered, left the dorm or eaten something more than chips from the vending machine. She was strung out and pissed off at her boyfriend, a bad combination. But despite the state she was in and her usually reliable preoccupation with herself, she took one look at Jacob, and she grabbed his hand and pulled him into her room.

"What the hell is going on?" she asked, while hugging him.

He pulled away and sat on her bed. "Where's your roommate?" he asked as he pulled a packet of cigarettes out of his pocket and tried to light one. (It took three matches before he was able to light it.)

"She's away; she's away somewhere for Spring break. I told you that. Everyone is fucking away. I've been stuck here like a loser," she said as she sat down on the bed opposite Jacob. "You can't smoke in here; the Gestapo will come in and like throw me out or something," she continued.

"I thought you said everyone was away," he said anxiously while exhaling a big cloud of smoke.

"Yeah but like there are sprinklers or some shit, and some RA prick, you just can't, you just can't smoke here," she said rubbing her eyes.

He took another deep drag and then dropped the burning cigarette into an empty diet Coke can on the floor nearby. It made a sizzling sound as the cigarette hit the flat soda.

Tash got up and walked over to Jacob. She sat down next to him. He put his head on her shoulder and softly said, "I need to crash here for a while, ok?"

"Yeah, ok. My roommate is coming back soon, I think like tomorrow or the next day," she said. "Jacob, what's going on?"

"Nothing, I just need to stay here and figure some stuff out, ok?"

"Tell me what's going on; you're really freaking me out," she fumed. "And I'm still mad at you for ditching me."

There was a long pause, and Jacob started to cry. Tash was taken back. Despite the fact that she was clearly ill-equipped to help anyone, she tried. She rubbed his back and in a much milder tone said, "It's ok. Whatever it is, it's ok. Tell me what's going on." And so he did. He told her everything.

They spent the next twenty-four hours brainstorming. Tash thought that maybe it wouldn't be so bad if he just went back to his apartment and then back to work. He could act like he didn't know anything about it. When he refuted that idea she suggested that he could explain what happened and work something out with whomever the drugs belonged to. She offered to try and get some money from her parents. She promised him that she was good at coming up with reasons they needed to send money. But he didn't think she could possibly get enough. She wanted to call Kyle for help; she trusted him, but Jacob made her swear up and down that she wouldn't tell a soul. By the next night he was convinced that he needed to get out of town. But that night as they were falling asleep in her small bed, she muttered, "What about your brother?"

Jacob hadn't even realized that he had left Melville in the apartment. "Shit," he said. "Shit, I forgot about him. I was so fucked when I was leaving."

"Call him, tell him he needs to get out of there," Tash whispered.

"He won't answer the phone," Jacob said.

"Doesn't he have a cell or email or something?" Tash asked.

"No, he doesn't have anything and I told him to never answer the apartment phone," Jacob said. He then continued, "I'll try, I'll try in the morning. I'll shout into the machine and maybe he'll pick up."

Tash and Jacob didn't wake up until two in the afternoon the next day. Groggy and out of it, it took Jacob nearly an hour to remember that he needed to call his brother. He called the apartment at least half a dozen times screaming into the machine for Melville to pick up, but he never answered. Melville was in the city hanging out with Pete at the teahouse.

"Shit," Jacob muttered to himself, as Tash came out of her bathroom in a white robe with a towel around her hair. "It feels good to be clean," she said before noticing how distressed Jacob looked. "What is it?" she asked.

"I can't get a hold of Melville. I called like a million times but he won't answer. I knew he wouldn't. Fuck! Fuck!" he screamed.

"Hey, don't worry about it," Tash said, walking over to comfort him. "I'm sure he'll be fine. He didn't do anything, and he doesn't know anything. I wouldn't freak out about it."

"I can't just leave him there Tash. I mean, I can't just fucking leave him there. I don't know what's gonna happen," Jacob said, holding his head in his hands.

"Well, what do you want to do?" she asked as she started to towel dry her long hair.

"I gotta go back to the apartment, just to tell him to get out of there," Jacob replied.

"Are you sure that's a good idea?" Tash asked.

"There's nothing else I can do. I'll go there and watch the building to make sure there's no one weird hanging around and I'll go in fast and tell him to get out."

Without hesitation Tash said, "I'll go with you."

"No, I don't think that's a good idea."

"I'm going with you. I have a bunch of stuff in your apartment. Besides, no one's gonna do anything to a girl. I'd be a good look-out or distraction or whatever if you need it."

Jacob was too worked up to think clearly so he just said, "Ok, ok you can come but we're gonna be fast, we're not gonna spend time packing all your stuff."

"Fine, I'll just grab my things while you get your brother. We'll be in and out in five minutes," Tash assured him.

*

Melville had met Pete at the teahouse at 11 o'clock that morning. They drank coffee and Melville listened to Pete go on and on about an exhibit at the MOMA that he just "must see." They grabbed a quick bite for lunch at a local deli where, per usual, they squabbled over the bill. Melville wanted to pay only for his tuna sandwich, and Pete wanted to split the bill down the middle. Then Pete told Melville that he had to leave for some plans he had. Melville headed back to his apartment by train. When Melville finally entered his apartment he walked over to the refrigerator, opened it up and took out a small bottle of Orangina. He flipped the cap off and walked into his bedroom, shutting the door behind him. He put his Orangina on his desk, took off his coat and slung it over the corner of his chair. He took a book off of his desk. He lay down on his couch with his head propped up against the pillow and began to read. He left his shoes on.

He had been reading for about 20 minutes when there was loud knocking on the door to the apartment. He ignored it assuming that, as always, either Jacob or Jeremy would get it. Soon the knocking turned into thumping. Melville dog-eared the page he was on and put his book down on his desk. He went and knocked on Jacob's door and when there was no answer he made his way to the front door, sure it was Jacob who was prone to forgetting his keys. He opened the door and two large men in black leather jackets shoved him into the apartment. He stumbled backwards and then found his footing. In shock, he just stood there as they closed the door behind them.

"Where is it?" they demanded. "Where the fuck is it?" Melville just shook his head, having no idea what was going on or what to say. "Come on guy, don't play stupid. We want our loot, and we want the candy shop open for business." Melville just stood there shaking his head, which enraged the two men. One said to the other, "Do you believe this guy playing stupid?" before he turned back to Melville. "We want the candy shop open, you got it?" When Melville didn't respond the two men started to walk slowly towards him, forcing him to walk backwards. He fell back onto the round kitchen table, leaning as far back as he could while the two men leaned over him. They were about to give him one last warning before they left but Melville didn't know what was going on and what they were going to do. He reached backward and grabbed the first thing he could feel, a small bottle top from his Orangina. He lunged forward to jam it in one of the guy's eyes, but failed. Then he tried to run away. Confused, he ran into his bedroom and was trying to lock the door when the two men entered. One grabbed him screaming on top of his lungs, "What the fuck was that? What the fuck is wrong with you?" Melville tried to push back, which caused the man who was holding him to throw him. As Melville tumbled through the air and over his couch he had one clear thought: it was finally getting warmer in his little room. He was relieved. As he finished this thought he smacked his head on the corner of his desk and fell to the floor, lifeless. There was blood pouring out from the side of his head.

"Oh fuck Marve," one of the men said to the one who had thrown Melville. "We were just supposed to get the store back open for business. Now we gotta fucking deal with this mess."

"He fell, he just fell," Marve said, seemingly shocked.

"Well, let's deal with this mess and get the hell out of here."

The two men searched the apartment for something they could put Melville in. With little to choose from, they took comforters from the two other bedrooms, wrapped Melville up, and headed out. On the way out, Marve said, "We should make it look like a break in," so they broke a couple of chairs, flung the kitchen cabinet doors open and jimmied the lock to the front door.

An hour later Jacob and Tash arrived at the apartment. Jacob panicked as soon as he saw the apartment door ajar. He pushed the door open telling Tash to "stay back." He walked in slowly, and Tash followed, closing the door behind her. The place was in disarray but he had left in such a hurry and haze that he thought he might have made the mess himself. "Mel," he said softly. "I'll go grab some stuff from your room," Tash said. "Mel," Jacob said a little louder. He made his way to Melville's room, knocked on the door and then twisted the door knob. He slowly opened the door hoping to find Melville lying on his couch with his earphones on. "Oh my God," he screamed, seeing the blood all over the desk. He ran over and saw a small pool of blood on the floor too. "Oh my God, oh my God. What have I done? What have I done?" he was repeating over and over again when Tash entered the room. He fell to his knees. "Look! Look at this. Oh my God," Jacob continued, now crying and bobbing back and forth on the ground. "Oh shit Jacob," Tash said in a panic. "We gotta go. We gotta get out of here."

Jacob was inconsolable so Tash walked over and bent down grabbing his head. "We've got to get the fuck out of here. Now Jacob, now."

"But, but, maybe we should call the police or, or…" Jacob wasn't able to find the words.

"What? Are you going to tell them what you think happened?" Tash paused, "Jacob, we don't even know what did happen. Maybe it looks worse than it is. And there's nothing you can do for him now. We've got to get out of here."

Wiping the tears from his face, he nodded in agreement.

"I'm gonna get my stuff from your room, and I'll try to grab some of your things too. You can't come back here; maybe you should see if there's anything else you really need," she said as she left the room.

Jacob sat staring at the blood and then decided to take some of Melville's things in case Tash was right and Melville was all right. He grabbed a small egg crate from under Melville's desk, flipped it over and put some things in it. He took a stack of notebooks and loose papers as well as some CDs from the desk. Then he went into his room and threw a jacket with a bag of weed in one of the pockets on top of the egg crate. Tash was standing with some clothes flung over one of her arms and a small backpack overflowing with Jacobs' things. They took what they had and left the apartment in silence.

*

On the train back, Jacob sat with the egg create on his lap, shaking the whole way. Tash tried to comfort him by rubbing his shoulder, but he barely even noticed. As they were approaching the city Tash asked, "What are you going to do?"

"I've got to get out of here. I'm going to call Mel's best friend, Pete, and see if I can leave Mel's stuff with him just in case Mel is ok and he comes back. But I've got to get out of here."

"Do you want to stay with me for a while until you figure things out?" Tash asked.

He shook his head. "I've got to get out of New York for a while."

Tash didn't respond, but the look on her face said that she understood. "Do me a favor," Jacob said as he turned to face Tash. "Will you look through the papers in here and see if you can find one with a guy named Pete's phone number?" he asked, holding the egg crate out.

"Sure," she said as she took the crate and put it on her lap. A minute later she was holding up a coffee shop napkin with Pete's name and phone number scribbled on it.

"Thanks," Jacob muttered as he took the napkin and put it in his pants pocket before taking the crate back. "I'll get off with you. Then I'm going to call this guy from a payphone and see if he can take this stuff."

"If he can't, I can keep it for you. Maybe you'll come back and you'll want to go through it all," Tash said sweetly.

"Thanks Babe, but I don't think you should have anything from me lying around right now."

She nodded.

A little while later they were standing on a crowded street. Jacob put the crate down to hug Tash. They squeezed each other tightly.

"Look me up when you come back," she whispered to him. "Yeah, will do. And take care of yourself. Get your stuff together so you don't, so you don't end up like…" but Tash interrupted, "Yeah, I know." Then she pulled away and gave him one last model pose, throwing her arms up in the air and exclaiming, "New adventures; don't let the party end!" She then sauntered off as he bent over to pick up the crate, while struggling to keep his overloaded backpack from slipping off his shoulder.

CHAPTER 18

Two hours later, Pete met Jacob at a local diner. Pete didn't know what to make of the frantic phone call, but when Jacob insisted he come and meet him regarding Melville's safety, he agreed. By the time Pete arrived, Jacob had been sitting in a booth, beside the egg crate, drinking black coffee loaded with sugars for nearly two hours. The only reason he hadn't been asked to leave was because it was off hours and the place wasn't crowded. Although the two had never met, they recognized each other immediately. Jacob waved Pete over.

"Hey man," he said as he sat down opposite Jacob. "Fuck, I know I don't know what you normally look like, but you look like hell man," Pete said with his characteristic near laugh and no-holds barred attitude. "So what's this all about. What's wrong with Melville?" Pete asked as he raised his arm to the waitress and mouthed the word "coffee."

After taking a few deep breaths Jacob began. He told Pete everything and begged him not to tell anyone. Quite uncharacteristically, Pete sat quietly and mostly just listened. Each time the waitress came over to refill their coffee cups, Jacob stopped talking.

Blown away, Pete could only say, "Wow, wow. That's a mind blow. Poor Melville. I can't believe it."

"I'm getting out of town tonight. I have some of Mel's things here, and I thought I would leave them with you, you know, in case. If that's all right. I don't know what else to do."

"Well, sure, sure you can leave them with me but don't you think you'd be better off leaving it with your cousin? He's probably more likely to call him, don't you think?" Pete asked.

Jacob had a puzzled look on his face. "We don't have any cousins. What are you talking about?" he asked.

"Your cousin. You know. Melville was always coming into the city to see him. That's how he and I would usually hook up and hang

183

out, after he had visited his cousin. Are you two like step brothers or something?" Pete asked jokingly.

Jacob just shook his head. "Dude, I don't know what Mel told you, but we don't have any cousins. Our parents don't have siblings. We don't have any family in New York at all. You must have misheard him or something."

Pete didn't know what to make of it, but he agreed to take Melville's belongings, and he wished Jacob good luck.

*

Prilly was just getting home from work when she heard her phone ringing. She let the machine get it but stopped in her tracks when she heard Pete's voice. She knew she had the willpower to resist the urge to pick up the phone; if she could do it before she could do it again. But when Pete said that something really, really awful had happened to Melville and that he needed to speak with her, she gave in and picked up the phone. He begged her to come to his apartment. When she refused, he told her he thought Melville was dead and that he needed her. "Please, please Prill, please come over." She agreed. She changed into tight dark blue jeans and a flowing gray baby-doll top, fixed her makeup and took a cab to his apartment. She arrived an hour after he had called.

She was excited, nervous and unsure of what she was doing. Her hands were trembling as she rang the buzzer. As she approached his apartment, the scene of so many heartbreaking and exhilarating moments, he opened the door, gave her a closed-mouthed smile, and said, "Come on in," in his sexiest voice. She sat on the chair by his desk and watched him open a bottle of wine in the kitchen. "I think I remembered you liked Chianti, right?" he asked. "Actually I like Cabernet," Prilly said. "Oh, that's right," he said blushing, "Well this is fabulous. You'll love it. I'm sure it's better than what you normally have."

"Pete, what's going on? I didn't come for a social call. You said Melville might be dead. Were you exaggerating? What are you talking about? What do you mean *might*?"

He walked over and handed her a glass and then went and sat in his bed and took a sip from his own glass. Then he told her about the call from Melville's brother, everything Jacob told him and how he gave him a box full of Melville's things, just in case. Prilly couldn't believe it. It was just too awful. She suddenly felt very ashamed of how she had treated Melville; she had always suspected he had a little crush on her.

As Prilly sat there trying to process all of it, Pete got up and went to the closet. He opened it up and took out a crate which he then placed on the bed. "That's it. Those are his things. Not much really, poor guy."

"May I?" Prilly asked, indicating she wanted to look in the box.

"Be my guest," Pete said.

As Prilly started to flip through the papers (notes about book titles, flyers to local events, some backdated unpaid bills) Pete said, "You know, the weirdest part is something Jacob said to me. He said Melville didn't have any cousins. But that's why he always told me he was in the city. I would bump into him at the teahouse, and he'd tell me he had come into the city to see his cousin. I don't get it," he said shaking his head and then taking another sip of his wine.

"He was coming to see you. He must have been coming to see you, and he felt embarrassed or something to say so," Prilly instantly said, now flipping through his notebooks and remembering how she had once seen him writing in one.

"Wow, you think so? Geeze. What a mindfuck. That's kind of sweet but also really sad, don't you think?" Pete asked.

"I don't know, I guess so," Prilly said. "Have you looked through these? It looks like he was writing a book or something," she continued, holding up one of the notebooks.

Pete shook his head. "I can't imagine it's very good," he said with a laugh. "I know it's terrible to say now but Melville didn't have an original thought in his life. That's probably why he was so fascinated with me."

"Uh, huh," Prilly said, captivated by what she was reading and wanting to tell Pete he was a jerk.

"Listen, Prilly," Pete said, trying to get her attention, "I've missed you. I've missed you a lot and I think..." but Prilly cut him off. "Pete, please. Don't. I came because you said something horrible happened to Melville but don't read anything else into it. I can't go there again."

"Ah, but you wouldn't have come if you didn't still have feelings for me. You know it's true. So it's silly to be stubborn about it..." but again, Prilly interrupted him. "Pete, I'm going to go. You seem ok and I'm not going to do this with you. I'm just not. I just can't."

With that she got up and turned to leave. Then she turned to face Pete and asked, "What are you going to do with those things?"

"I don't know. I guess I'll just stick them in the closet," he said, shrugging his shoulders.

"Well if you're just going to do that do you mind if I take the notebooks. I'd like to read what he wrote. I can send them back to you if you want."

"Sure, sure, you can take them," Pete said. "You'll be disappointed my dear, but suit yourself. Keep 'em."

With that Prilly took the notebooks out of the crate and headed to the front door. Pete followed her and put his hand out, shutting the door just before she walked out. She turned around, pressed firmly between Pete and the door. He leaned in to kiss her but she turned her head. He pulled back and she said, "I really hope Melville turns up and that he's all right." Then she walked out of the apartment.

During the cab ride home she felt a slew of emotions. She felt sad for Melville, vindicated that Pete still wanted her and both pride and pain at having to walk away. But more than ever before, the things he said and the way he said them had made her think that he wasn't capable of caring about anyone except for himself, and she knew that would never work for her. He was so arrogant, and, for once, looking around that dingy little apartment, she couldn't quite figure out why. That night, she lay on her couch reading Melville's notebooks, which were a mix of memoir and fantasy with some mindless ramblings interspersed throughout. But there was a story in it all. It was a story about a shy and lonely man who longed to be all that he wasn't. She found it quite beautiful.

*

The next morning Janice was brewing her decaf when Kyle came into the kitchen to grab an energy drink. "You're up early," she said, surprised to see him.

"Yeah, I'm meeting a friend for breakfast before school."

"Oh," Janice said, as she started to pour a cup of coffee. "Well don't be late for school."

"Don't worry. I have a study hall first period."

"Who are you meeting, Sam?" she asked before taking her first sip of coffee.

"No, just a friend who was having some problems. She is better though, I think, and I'm just checking up on her."

"That's nice Honey," Janice said before placing her cup on the counter. "Kyle," she called as he was halfway through the dining room.

"Yeah Mom?" he paused and asked.

"It's nice how you look out for your friends. It's very nice... My mother is like that... That's all... I just wanted to say that."

Kyle walked back to her and gave her a kiss on her forehead. He smiled and left, hollering, "Have a great day," before shutting the front door.

She enjoyed another sip of her coffee and then noticed her Blackberry was vibrating in her suit pocket. She took it out and scrolled to her new emails. There was a new email from Prilly that read:

Janice: On my way to pick up the posters. See you at the convention center. Prilly.

Janice slipped her Blackberry into her pocket, leaned against the kitchen counter and finished her cup of coffee while admiring the ivory molding, framing the kitchen doorway.

ABOUT THE AUTHOR

Patricia Leavy is Associate Professor of Sociology and the Founding Director of Gender Studies (2004-2008) at Stonehill College in Easton, Massachusetts. Leavy has emerged as a leader in the qualitative and arts-based research communities. She is the author of *Essentials of Transdisciplinary Research Practice: Using Problem-Centered Methodologies* (Left Coast Press, forthcoming); *Oral History: Understanding Qualitative Research* (Oxford University Press, 2011); *Method Meets Art: Arts-Based Research Practice* (Guilford Press, 2009); and *Iconic Events: Media, Politics and Power in Retelling History* (Lexington Books, 2007). She is coauthor of *The Practice of Qualitative Research* 1st and 2nd editions (Sage Publications, 2005, 2011) and *Feminist Research Practice: A Primer* (Sage, 2007). She is the editor of *The Oxford Handbook of Qualitative Research* (Oxford University Press, forthcoming) and the co-editor of *Hybrid Identities: Theoretical and Empirical Examinations* (Haymarket, 2008); *Handbook of Emergent Methods* (Guilford Press, 2008); *Emergent Methods in Social Research* (Sage, 2006) and *Approaches to Qualitative Research: A Reader on Theory and Practice* (Oxford University Press, 2004). In addition to serving as the editor for the *Social Fictions* book series with Sense Publishers, she is also serving as the editor for the Oxford University Press book series *Understanding Qualitative Research*. She is regularly quoted in national and local newspapers for her expertise on popular culture, gender and other sociological topics. She has appeared on television programs including CNN's "Glenn Beck Show" and "Lou Dobbs Tonight." The New England Sociological Association named Leavy the 2010 "New England Sociologist of the Year." She is also a published poet. For more information please visit www.patricialeavy.com.

CPSIA information can be obtained at www.ICGtesting.com
Printed in the USA
BVOW021552130612

292563BV00002B/1/P